Treasure of Ambedkar Series 02

FEDERATION VERSUS FREEDOM

Dr B.R. Ambedkar

KALPAZ

Treasure of Ambedkar Series 02

FEDERATION VERSUS FREEDOM

ISBN: 978-93-5128-269-3

First Published 1939
Reprint **2017**, in India by
Kalpaz Publications
C-30, Satyawati Nagar,
Delhi – 110052
E-mail: kalpaz@hotmail.com
Ph.: 9212142040

Printed at: G. Print Process, Delhi

CONTENTS.

PREFACE V

I. INTRODUCTORY. 1

II. BIRTH AND GROWTH OF THE FEDERATION. 3

III. STRUCTURE OF THE FEDERATION. . . . 13

IV. POWERS OF THE FEDERATION. 25

V. CHARACTER OF THE FEDERATION. . . .38

VI. BENEFITS OF THE FEDERATION SCHEME 71

VII. THE BANE OF THE FEDERATION. 101

VIII. FATALITY OF THE FEDERATION. 125

IX. FEDERATION WITHOUT THE STATES. 132

X. FEDERATION FROM DIFFERENT POINTS OF VIEW. 145

XI. CONCLUSION. 152

PREFACE.

A word or two as regards the origin of this tract and the motive which has led me to publish it at this time will, I think, not be out of place.

Many in this country must be aware that there exists in Poona an institution which is called the GOKHALE INSTITUTE of POLITICS and ECONOMICS, working under the direction of Dr. D.R. GADGIL. The Institute holds a function annually to celebrate what is called the Founder's Day and invites some one to deliver an address on some subject connected with politics or economics. This year, I was asked by Dr. GADGIL to deliver an address. I accepted the invitation and chose the Federal Scheme as the subject of my address. The address covered both (1) the structure of the Federation and (2) a critique of that structure. The address was delivered on 29th January 1939 at the Gokhale Hall in Poona. The address as prepared had become too lengthy for the time allotted to me and although I kept the audience for two hours when usually the time allotted for such addresses is one hour I had to omit from the address the whole of the part relating to the Federal structure and some portion from the part relating to the criticism of the structure. This tract, however, contains the whole of the original address prepared by me for the occasion.

So much for the origin of this tract. Now as to the reasons for publishing it. All addresses delivered at the Gokhale Institute are published. It is in the course of things that this also should be published. But there are other reasons besides this, which have prevailed with me to publish it. So far as the Federation is concerned, the generality of the Indian public seems to be living in a fog. Beyond the fact that there is to be a Federation and that the Federation is a bad thing the general public has no clear conception of what is the nature of this Federation and is, therefore, unable to form an intelligent opinion about it. It is necessary that the general public should have in its hand a leaflet containing an outline of the Federal structure and a criticism of that structure in small compass sufficient to convey a workable understanding of the Scheme. I feel this Tract will supply this need.

I also think that the publication of this tract will be regarded as timely. Federation is a very live issue and it is also a very urgent one. Soon the people of British India will be called upon to decide whether they should accept the Federal Scheme or they should not. The premier political organization in this Country, namely, the Congress seems to be willing to accept this Federation as it has accepted Provincial Autonomy. The negotiations that are going on with the Muslim League and the manoeuvres that are being carried on with the Indian States give me at any rate the impression that the Congress is prepared to accept the Federation and that these negotiations and manoeuvres are designed to bring about a working arrangement with other parties so that with their help the Congress may be in the saddle at the Centre as it has been in the Provinces. Mr. Subhas Chandra Bose has even gone to the length of suggesting that the right wing of the Congress has committed itself to this Federation so far that it has already selected its cabinet. It matters not whether all this is true or not. I hope all this is untrue. Be that as it may, the matter is both grave and urgent, and I think all those who have anything to say on the subject should speak it out. Indeed I feel that silence at such a time will be criminal. That is why I have hastened to publish my address. I believe that I have views on the subject of Federation which even if they do not convince others will at least provoke them to think.

1-3-39
Rajgraha
Dadar, Bombay, 14

B. R. Ambedkar.

I. INTRODUCTORY.

Dr. Gadgil and students of the Gokhale Institute,

I feel greatly honoured by your invitation to address you this evening. You have met today to celebrate a day which is set out as your Founder's Day. I had the privilege of personally knowing the late Rao Bahadur R. R. Kale the founder of your Institute. He was my colleague in the old Bombay Legislative Council. I know how much care and study he used to bestow upon every subject which he handled. I am sure he deserves the gratitude of all those who care for knowledge and study for helping to establish this Institute, whose main function as I understand is to dig for knowledge and make it ready for those who care to use it. For, first, knowledge is power as nothing else is, and secondly, not all those who wish and care for knowledge have the leisure and the patience to dig for it. As one who believes in the necessity of knowledge and appreciates the difficulties in its acquisition I am glad to be associated in this way with him and with the Institute he has founded.

The theme I have chosen for the subject matter of my address is the Federal Scheme embodied in the Government of India Act, 1935. The title of the subject might give you the impression that I am going to explain the Federal Constitution. That would be an impossible task in itself. The Federal Scheme is a vast thing. Its provisions are contained, first in 321 sections of the Government of India Act, 1935, secondly in in the 9 Schedules which are part of the Act, thirdly in 31 Orders-in-Council issued under the Act and fourthly the hundreds of Instruments of Accessions to be passed by the Indian States. Very few can claim mastery over so vast a subject and if any did he would take years to expound it in all its details. I have set to myself a very limited task. It is to examine the scheme in the light of certain accepted tests and to place before you the results of this examination so that you may be in a position to form your own judgment regarding the merits of the scheme. It is true that I cannot altogether avoid setting out the outlines of the scheme. In fact, I am going to give an outline of the scheme. I realize that it is an essential preliminary without which my criticism might remain high up in the air. But the outline I am going to draw for my purpose will be the briefest and just enough to enable you to follow what I shall be saying regarding the merits of the scheme.

II. BIRTH AND GROWTH OF THE INDIAN FEDERATION.

There are five countries which are known in modern times to have adopted the federal form of Government. They are: (1) U. S. A., (2) Switzerland, (3) Imperial Germany, (4) Canada and (5) Australia. To these five it is now proposed to add the sixth which is this All—India Federation.

What are the constituent units of this Federation? For an answer to this question refer to Section 5. It says:—

"5. (1) It shall be lawful for His Majesty, if an address in that behalf has been presented to him by each House of Parliament and if the condition hereinafter mentioned is satisfied, to declare by Proclamation that as from the day therein appointed there shall be united in a Federation under the Crown, by the name of the Federation of India,

Proclamation of Federation of India.

(a) The Provinces hereinafter called Governors' Provinces; and

(b) the Indian States which have acceded or may thereafter accede to the Federation;

and in the Federation so established there shall be included the Provinces hereinafter called Chief Commissioners' Provinces.

(2) The condition referred to is that States—

(a) the Rulers whereof will, in accordance with the provision contained in Part II of the First Schedule to this Act, be entitled to choose not less than fifty-two members of the Council of State; and

(b) the aggregate population whereof, as ascertained in accordance with the said provisions, amounts to at least one-half of the total population of States as so ascertained, have acceded to the Federation."

Leaving aside the conditions prescribed by this section for the inauguration of the Federation it is clear that the Units of the Federation are (1) The Governors' Provinces, (2) Chief Commissioner's Provinces and (3) The Indian States.

What is the size of this Indian Federation?

Many people when they speak of the Indian Federation do not seem to realize what an enormous entity it is going to be.

	Population	Area	Units.
U. S. A. ...	122,775,040	2,973,773	48 States plus 1 Federal Dist.
Germany ...	67,000,000	208,780	25 ...
Switzerland ...	4,66,400	15,976	22 ...
Canada ...	10,376,786	3,729,665	9 ...
Australia ...	6,629,839	2,974,581	6 ...
India ...	352,837,778	1,808,679	162 ...

The Indian Federation in point of area is 3/5th of U. S. A. and of Australia and half of Canada. It is 9 times of Germany and 120 times of Switzerland. In point of population it is 3 times of U.S.A., 5 times of Germany, 35 times of Canada, 58 times of Australia and 88 times of Switzerland. Measured by the Units which compose it, it is 3 times larger than U. S. A., 6½ times larger than Germany, 8 times larger than Switzerland, 18 times larger than Canada and 27 times larger than Australia. Thus the Indian Federation is not merely a big federation. It is really a monster among federations.

What is the source from which the Federation derives its Governmental Powers and Authority?

Section 7 says that the executive authority of the Federation shall be exercised on behalf of His Majesty by the Governor-General. That means that the Authority of the Federation is derived from the Crown. In this respect the Indian Federation differs from the Federation in the U. S. A. In the U. S. A., the powers of the Federation are derived from the people. The people of the United States are the fountain from which the authority is derived. While it differs from the Federation in the U. S. A. the Indian Federation resembles the Federations in Australia and Canada. In Australia and Canada the source of the Authority for the Federal Government is also the Crown and

Section 7 of the Government of India Act is analogous to Section 61 of the Australian Act and Section 9 of the Canadian Act. That the Indian Federation should differ in this respect from the American Federation and agree with the Canadian and Australian Federation is perfectly understandable. The United States is a republic while Canada, Australia and India are dominions of the Crown. In the former the source of all authority are the people. In the latter the source of all authority is the Crown.

From where does the Crown derive its authority?

Such a question is unnecessary in the case of Canada and Australia, because the Crown is the ultimate source of all authority and there is nothing beyond or behind, to which his authority is referable. Can this be said of the Indian Federation? Is the Crown the ultimate source of authority exercised by the Federation? Is there nothing beyond or behind the Crown to which this authority needs to be referred? The answer to this question is that only for a part of the authority of the Federation the Crown is the ultimate source and that for the remaining part the Crown is not the ultimate source.

That this is the true state of affairs is clear from the terms of the Instrument of Accession. I quote the following from the draft Instrument :—

> " Whereas proposals for the establishment of a Federation of India comprising such

Indian States as may accede thereto and the Provinces of British India constituted as Autonomous Provinces have been discussed between representatives of His Majesty's Government of the Parliament of the United Kingdom, of British India and of the Rulers of the Indian States ;

And Whereas those proposals contemplated that the Federation of India should be constituted by an Act of the Parliament of the United Kingdom and by the accession of Indian States :

And Whereas provision for the constitution of a Federation of India has now been made in the Government of India Act, 1935 ;

And Whereas that Act provided that the Federation shall not be established until such date as His Majesty may, by proclamation, declare, and such declaration cannot be made until the requisite number of Indian States have acceded to the Federation :

And Whereas the said Act cannot apply to any of my territories save by virtue of my consent and concurrence signified by my accession to the Federation ;

Now, therefore, I (insert full name and title), Ruler of (insert name of State), in the exercise of my sovereignty in and over my said State for the purpose of co-operating in the furtherance of the interests and welfare of India by uniting in a Federation under the Crown by the name of the Federation of India with Provinces called Governors' Provinces and with the Provinces called Chief Commissioners' Provinces and with the Rulers of other Indian States do hereby execute this my Instrument of Accession, and I hereby declare that subject to His Majesty's acceptance of this Instrument, I accede to the Federation of India as established under the Government of India Act, 1935."

This is a very important feature of the Indian Federation. What has brought about this difference between the Indian Federation and the Canadian and Australian Federation? For what part is the Crown the ultimate source and for what part is it not? To understand these questions you must take note of two things. First, the Indian Federation comprises two distinct areas: British India and Indian States. This will be clear if you refer to Section 5. Second, the relationship of these two areas with the Crown is not the same. The area known as British India is vested in the Crown while the area comprised in an Indian State is not vested in the Crown but is vested in the Ruler. This is clear if you refer to Sections 2 and 311. The territory of British India being vested in the Crown the sovereignty over it belongs to the Crown and the territory of an Indian State being vested in the Ruler of the State the sovereignty over the State belongs to the Ruler of the State.

You will now understand why I said that in the Indian Federation the Crown is the ultimate source for a part of its authority and for the remaining part the Crown is the ultimate source of authority of the Indian Federation in so far as British India is part of the Federation. The Indian Ruler is the ultimate source of authority in so far as his State is part of this Federation. When therefore Section 7 says that the Executive Authority of the Federation shall be exercised by the Governor-General on behalf of the Crown it must be understood that Crown's authority which is delegated by him to the Governor-General in the working out of the Indian Federation is partly its own and partly derived from the Rulers of the Indian State.

What is the process by which the Crown acquires the authority which belongs to the ruler of an Indian State ? The process is known under the India Act as Accession. This Accession is effected by what is called an Instrument of Accession executed by the Ruler of a state. The provisions relating to the Instrument of Accession are contained in Section 6 (1). That Section reads as follows :—

"6 A State shall be deemed to have acceded to the Federation if His Majesty has signified his acceptance of an Instrument of Accession executed by the Ruler thereof, whereby the Ruler for himself, his heirs and successors

(a) declares that he accedes to the Federation as established under this Act, with the intent that His Majesty the King, the Governor-General of India, the Federal Legislature, the Federal Court and any other Federal Authority established for the purposes of the Federation shall by virtue of his Instrument of Accession, but subject always to the terms thereof, and for the purposes only of the Federation, exercise in relation to his State such functions as may be vested in him by or under this Act ; and

(b) assumes the obligation of ensuring that due effect is given within his State to the provisions of this Act so far as they are applicable therein by virtue of his Instrument of Accession."

It is this Instrument of Accession which confers authority upon the Crown in the first instance so far as an Indian State is part of the Federation and it is because of this that the Crown's Authority in and over this Federation is derivative in part.

This is the law as to the birth of the Federation. What is the law as to the growth of this Federation ? In other words what is the law as to

change ? The law as to change is contained in Section 6 (1) (a), Schedule II and Section 6 (5).

Section 6 (1) (a) makes it clear that the accession by a Prince, effected through his Instrument of Accession, is "to the Federation as established by this Act." Schedule II deals with future amendment of the Constitution. It declares what are the provisions in the Government of India Act an amendment of which will be deemed to affect the Instrument of Accession and what are the provisions an amendment of which will not affect the Instrument of Accession by the States.

Section 6 (5) does two things. In the firs place it provides that the Instrument of Accessic shall be deemed to confer upon Parliament t right to amend these provisions which are decla by Schedule II as open to amendment witl affecting the Instrument of Accession. In second place it provides that although Parlia may amend a provision of the Act which is de by Schedule II as open to amendment v affecting the Instrument of Accession s amendment shall not bind the States unl accepted as binding by the State by a su tary Instrument of Accession.

" To sum up, the units of this Fed not form one single whole with a com of action. The units are separate. T held together. For some purposes th

the units cannot be altered at all. For some purposes alteration is permissible but such alteration cannot bind all the units alike. Some will be bound by it but some will not be unless they consent to be bound. In other words, in this Federation there is no provision for growth. It is fixed. It cannot move. A change by evolution is not possible and where it is possible it is not binding unless it is accepted.

III. THE STRUCTURE OF THE FEDERATION.

(a) The Federal Legislature.

The Federal Legislature is a bicameral legislature. There is a Lower House which is spoken of as the Legislative Assembly and there is an Upper House which is called the Council of State. The composition of the two Chambers is a noteworthy feature. They are very small Chambers compared with other legislatures having regard to the population and the area, as the total membership of the Federal Assembly is 375 and of the Council of State 260. These seats are divided in a certain proportion between British India and the Indian States. Of the 375 seats in the Federal Assembly 250 are allotted to British India and 125 to the Indian States. In the Council of State, out of the 260 seats, 156 are allotted to British India and 104 to the Indian States. It may be noticed that this distribution between British India and the Indian States is not based upon an equalitarian principle. It is possible to take the population as the basis of representation. It is also possible to take the revenue as the basis of representation, but neither of these has been taken as the basis of distribution of seats. Whether you take population as the basis or whether you take revenue as the basis, you will find that British India has been under-represented, while the Indian States have been over-represented in the two Chambers. The method of filling the seats is also noteworthy. The respresentatives of the British India in both the Chambers will be elected. The representatives of the Indian States, on the other hand, are to be appointed, i. e., nominated, by the Rulers of the States. It is open to a Ruler to provide that the representatives of his State, though appointed by him, may be chosen by his subjects, but this is a matter which is left to his discretion. He may appoint a person who is chosen by his people or he may, if he pleases, do both, choose and appoint. In the final result a State's representative is to be appointed by the Ruler as distinguished from being elected by the people. In the case of British India, the representatives are to be elected, but here again there is a peculiarity which may be noticed. In the case of all bi-cameral Legislatures the Lower House being a popular house is always elected directly by the people, while the Upper House being a revising Chamber is elected by indirect election. In the case of the Indian Federation this process is reversed. The Upper Chamber will be elected by direct election by the people and it is the Lower Chamber which is going to be elected indirectly by the Provincial Legislatures. The life of the Federal Assembly is fixed for a term of five years, although it may be dissolved sooner. The Council of State on the other hand is a permanent body not liable to dissolution. It is a body which lives by renewal of a third part of its membership every three years.

Now the authority of the two Chambers to pass laws and to sanction expenditure may be noted. With regard to the authority to pass laws some constitutions make a distinction between money bills and other bills and provide that with regard to money bills the Upper Chamber shall not have the power to initiate such a bill, and also that the Upper Chamber shall not have the authority to reject it. It is given the power only to suspend the passing of the bill for a stated period. The Indian constitution makes no such distinction at all. The money bills and other bills are treated on the same footing and require the assent of both the Chambers before they can become law. The only distinction is that while according to Sec. 30 (1) a bill which is not a money bill may originate in either Chamber, a money bill, according to Section 37, shall not originate in the Upper Chamber. But according to Section 30 (2) a money bill needs the assent of the Upper Chamber as much as any other bill.

With regard to the authority to sanction expenditure: here again there is a departure made in the accepted principles of distributing authority between the two Chambers when a Legislature is bi-cameral.

According to Section 31 (1) the Annual Financial Statement of estimated receipts and expenditure shall be laid before both Chambers of the Federal Legislature and shall, of course, be open to discussion in both the Chambers. Not only are they open to discussion in both the Chambers, they are also subject to the vote of both the Chambers. Section 34 (2) requires that the expenditure shall be submitted in the form of demands for grants to the Federal Assembly and thereafter to the Council of State and either Chamber shall have the power to assent to or refuse any demand, or to assent to any demand subject to a reduction of the amount specified therein.

It will thus be seen that the two Chambers are co-equal in authority, both in the matter of their authority to pass laws and in the matter of sanctioning expenditure. A conflict between the two Chambers cannot end by one Chamber yielding to the other if that Chamber does not wish so to yield. The procedure adopted for the resolving of differences between the two Chambers is the method of joint sessions. Sec. 31 (1) deals with the procedure with regard to joint sessions where the conflict relates to a bill. Sec. 34 (3) relates to the procedure where the conflict relates to the differences with regard to sanctioning of expenditure.

(b) The Federal Executive.

The constitution of the Federal Executive is described in Sec. 7 (I). According to this section the executive Authority of the Federation is handed over to the Governor-General. It is he who is the Executive Authority for the Federation. The first thing to note about this Federal Executive is that it is a unitary executive and not a corporate body. In India ever since the British took up the civil and military government of the country, the executive has never been unitary in composition. The executive was a composite executive. In the Provinces it was known as the Governor-in-Council. At the Centre it was known as the Governor-General-in-Council. The civil and military government of the Provinces as well as of India was not vested either in the Governor or in the Governor-General. The body in which it was vested was the Governor with his Councillors. The Councillors were appointed by the King and did not derive their authority from the Governor or from the Governor-General. They derived their authority from the Crown and possessed co-equal authority with the Governor and the Governor-General and, barring questions where the peace and tranquility of the territory was concerned, the Governor and the Governor-General were bound by the decision of the majority. The constitution, therefore, makes a departure from the established system. I am not saying that this departure is unsound in principle or it is not justified by precedent or by the circumstances arising out of the necessities of a federal constitution. All I want you to note is that this is a very significant change.

The next thing to note about the Federal Executive is that although the Governor-General is the Executive Authority for the Federation, there are conditions laid down for the exercise of his powers as the Federal Executive. The constitution divides the matters falling within his executive authority into four classes and prescribes how he is to exercise his executive authority in respect of each of these four classes. In certain matters the Governor-General (1) is to act in his own discretion ; (2) in certain matters he is to act on the advice of his Ministers ; (3) in certain matters he is to act after consultation with his Ministers, and (4) in certain matters he is to act according to his individual judgment. A word may be said as to the *de-jure* connotation that underlies these four cases of the exercise of the executive authority by the Governor-General. The best way to begin to explain this *de jure* connotation is to begin by explaining what is meant by "acting on the advice of his ministers." This means, in those matters the government is really carried on, on the authority of the Ministers and only in the name of the Governor-General. To put the same thing differently, the advice of the Ministers is binding on the Governor-General and he cannot differ from their advice. With regard to the matters where the Governor-General is allowed "to act in his discretion" what is meant is that the Government is not only carried on in the name of the Governor-General, but is also carried on on the authority of the Governor-General. That means that there can be no intervention or interference by the Ministers at any stage. The Ministers have no right to tender any advice and the Governor-General is not bound to seek their advice; or to make it concrete, the files with regard to these matters need not go to the Ministers at all. "Acting in his individual judgment" means that while the matter is within the advisory jurisdiction of the Minister, the Minister has no final authority to decide. The final authority to decide is the Governor-General. The distinction between "in his discretion" and "in his individual judgment" is this, that while in regard to matters falling "in his discretion" the Ministers have no right to tender advice to the Governor-General, the Ministers have a right to tender advice when the matter is one which falls under "his individual judgment". To put it differently in regard to matters which are subject to his individual judgment the Governor-General is bound to receive advice from his ministers but is not bound to follow their advice. He may consider their advice, but may act otherwise and differently from the advice given by the

Ministers. But in respect of matters which are subject to his discretion he is not bound even to receive the advice of his Ministers. The phrase "after consultation" is a mere matter of procedure. The authority in such a matter vests in the Governor-General. All that is required is that he should take into account the wishes of the Ministers. Cases relating to "acting after consultation" may be distinguished from cases relating to "individual judgment" in this way. In cases relating to "individual judgment" the authority vests in the Ministers. The Governor-General has the power to superintend and, if necessary, overrule. In the cases falling under "after consultation", the authority belongs to the Governor-General and the Ministers have the liberty to say what they wish should be done.

(c) The Federal Judiciary.

The Government of India Act provides for the constitution of a Federal Court as part of the Federal Constitution. The Federal Court is to consist of a Chief Justice and such Puisne Judges as His Majesty thinks necessary, their number not to exceed six until an address is presented by the Legislature asking for an increase. The Federal Judiciary has original as well as appellate jurisdiction. Sec. 204, which speaks of the Original Jurisdiction of the Federal Court, prescribes that that Court shall have exclusive Original jurisdiction in any dispute between the Federation, the Provinces and the federated States which involves any question of law or fact on which the existence or extent of a legal right depends. This section, however, provides that if a State is party then the dispute must concern the interpretation of the Act or an Order in Council thereunder, or the extent of the legislative or executive authority vested in the Federation by the Instrument of Accession or arise under an Agreement under Part VI of the Act for the administration of a federal law in the States, or otherwise concern some matter in which the Federal Legislature has power to legislate for the States or arise under an agreement made after federation with the approval of the Representative of the Crown between the States and the Federation or a Province, and includes provision for such jurisdiction. Even this limited jurisdiction of the Federal Court over the States is further limited by the proviso that no dispute is justiciable if it arises under an agreement expressly excluding such jurisdiction.

The appellate jurisdiction of the Federal Court is regulated by Sections, 205 and Section 207 ; Section 205 says that an appeal shall lie to the Federal Court from any judgment, decree or final order of a High Court in British India if the High Court certified that the case involves a substantial question of law as to the interpretation of this Act or any Order in Council made thereunder. Section 207 relates to appeals from decision of Courts of the Federated States. It says that an appeal shall lie to the Federal Court from a Court in a federated State on the ground that a question of law has been wrongly decided, being a question which concerns the interpretation of this Act or of any Order in Council made thereunder or the extent of the legislative or executive authority vested in the Federation by virtue of the Instrument of Accession of that State or arises under an Agreement made under Part VI of this Act in relation to the administration in that State of a law of the Federal Legislature; but Sub-Section (2) to Section 207 provides that an appeal under this section shall be by way of a special case to be stated for the opinion of the Federal Court by a High Court, and the Federal Court may require a case to be so stated.

Two further points with regard to the Federal Judiciary may be noted. The first is the power of the Federal Court to execute its own orders. The Federal Court has no machinery of its own to enforce its orders. Sec. 210 provides that the orders of the Federal Court shall be enforceable by all courts and authorities in every part of British India or of any Federated State as if they were orders duly made by the highest court exercising civil or criminal jurisdiction as the case may be in that part. The instrumentality, therefore, which the Federal Court can use for the enforcemen tof its own orders consists of the administrative machinery of the units of the Federation. The units of the Federation are bound to act in aid of the Federal Court. This is different to what prevails for instance, in the United States of America, where the Supreme Court has its own machinery for enforcing its own orders.

The second point to note with regard to the Federal Court is the question of the powers of the Executive to remove the judges and the power of the Legislature to discuss their conduct. In this respect also the Federal Court stands on a different footing from the Federal Courts in other Federations. The Constitution does not give the Governor-General the power to suspend a Judge of the Federal Court. It forbids any discussion of a judge's judicial conduct by the Legislature. This, no doubt, gives the judge of the Federal Court the greatest fixity of tenure and immunity from interference by the Executive or by the Legislature. To remove the Judiciary from the control of the Executive it has been found necessary that the tenure of a judge must not be subject to the pleasure of the Excutive. All constitutions, therefore, provide that the tenure of a judge shall be during good behaviour and that a judge shall be removeable only if address is presented by the Legislature pronouncing that he is not of good behaviour. Some such authority must be vested in some body which should have the power to pronounce upon the good behaviour of a judge. This provision is absent in the Federal Constitution, so that a Judge of the Federal Court once appointed is irremoveable from his place till retirement, no matter what his conduct during that period may be. Instead of this, power is given to His Majesty under Sec. 200 (2) (b) to remove a Judge of the Federal Court on the ground of misbehaviour or infirmity of body or mind if the Judicial Committee of the Privy Council reports that he may be removed on any such ground.

IV. POWERS OF THE FEDERATION.

Before I describe the powers of the Federal Government it might be desirable to explain what is the essence of a Federal Form of Government. There is no simpler way of explaining it than by contrasting it with the Unitary Form of Government.

Although the Federal Form of Government is distinct from the Unitary form, it is not easy to see the distinction. On the other hand, there is, outwardly at any rate, a great deal of similarity between the two. The Government of almost every country in these days is carried on by an inter-related group of Administrative Units operating in specific areas and discharging specific public functions. This is true of a country with a Federal Form of Government and also of a country with a Unitary form of Government. In a Federal Constitution there is a Central Government and there are inter-related to it several Local Governments. In the same way in an Unitary Constitution there is a Central Government and there are inter-related to it several Local Governments. On the surface, therefore, there appears to be no difference between the two.

There is, however, a real difference between them although it is not obvious. That difference lies in the nature of the inter-relationship between the Central and the Local Administrative Units. This difference may be summed up in this way. In the Unitary Form of Government, the powers of the local bodies are derived from an Act of the Central Government. That being so the powers of the Local Government can always be withdrawn by the Central Government. In the Federal form of Government the powers of the Central Government as well as of the Local Government are derived by the.law of the Constitution which neither the Local Government nor the Central Government can alter by its own act. Both derive their powers from the law of the Constitution and each is required by the Constitution to confine itself to the powers given to it. Not only does the Constitution fix the powers of each but the constitution establishes a judiciary to declare any act whether of the Local or the Central Government as void if it transgresses the limits fixed for it by the Constitution. This is well stated by Clement in his volume on the Canadian Constitution in the following passage :-

"Apart from detail, the term federal union in these modern times implies an agreement........to commit......people to the control of one common government in relation to such matters as are agreed upon as of common concern, leaving each local government still independent and autonomous in all other matters, as a necessary corollary the whole arrangement constitutes a fundamental law to be recognised in and enforced through the agency of the Courts."

"The exact position of the line which is to divide matters of common concern to the whole federation from matters of local concern in each unit is not of the essence of federalism. Where it is to be drawn in any proposed scheme depends upon the view adopted by the federating communities as to what, in their actual circumstances, geographical, commercial, racial or otherwise, are really matters of common concern and as such proper to be assigned to a common government. But the maintenance of the line, as fixed by the federating agreement, is of the essence of modern federalism ; at least, as exhibited in the three great Anglo-Saxon federations of today, the United States of America, the Commonwealth of Australia, and the Dominion of Canada. Hence the importance and gravity of the duty thrown upon the Courts as the only constitutional interpreter of the organic instrument which contains the fundamental law of the land."

Thus to draw a line for the purpose of dividing the powers of Government between the Central and Local Governments by the law of the Constitution and to maintain that line through the judiciary are the two essential features of the Federal Form of

Government. It is these two features which distinguish it from the Unitary Form of Government. In short every federation involves two things. (1) Division of Powers by metes and bounds between the Central Government and the Units which compose it by the law of the Constitution, which is beyond the power of either to change and to limit the action of each to the powers given and (2) a Tribunal beyond the control of either to decide when the issue arises as to whether any particular act of the Centre or of the Unit, Legislative, Executive, Administrative or Financial is beyond the powers given to it by the Constitution.

Having explained what is meant by Federal Government, I will now proceed to give you some idea of the Powers which are assigned by the constitution to the Federal Government.

(a) Legislative Powers of the Federation.—

For the purposes of distributing the Legislative Powers the possible subjects of Legislation are listed into three categories. The first category includes subjects, the exclusive right to legislate upon which is given to the Federal Legislature. This list is called the Federal List. The second category includes subjects, the exclusive right to legislate upon which is given to the Provincial Legislature. This list is called the Provincial List. The third category includes subjects over which both the Federal as well as the Provincial Legislature have a right to legislate. This list is called the Concurrent list. The scope and contents of these lists are given in Schedule VII to the Government of India Act.

In accordance with the fundamental principles of Federation a law made by the Federal Legislature if it relates to a matter which is included in the Provincial List, would be *ultra vires* and a nullity. Similarly, if the Provincial Legislature were to make a law relating to a matter falling in the Federal List such a Provincial Law would be *ultra vires* and therefore a nullity. This is, however, declared by statute and Sec. 107 is now the law on the point. Cases of conflict of legislation touching the Federal List and the Provincial List are not likely to occur often. But cases of conflict between the two are sure to arise in the concurrent field of legislation. The law as to that you will find in Section 107. Sub-Section (1) lays down when a Federal Law shall prevail over a Provincial Law. Sub-Section (2) lays down as to when a Provincial Law shall prevail over the Federal Law. Reading the sub-sections together the position in law is this. As a rule a Federal Law shall prevail over a Provincial Law if the two are in conflict. But in cases where the Provincial Law, having been reserved for the consideration of the Governor-General or for the signification of His Majesty's pleasure, has received the assent of the Governor-

General or His Majesty, the Provincial Law shall prevail until the Federal Legislature enacts further legislation with respect to the same matter.

With regard to the question of this distribution of powers of legislation every Federation is faced with a problem. That problem arises because there can be no guarantee that enumeration of the subjects of legislation is exhaustive and includes every possible subject of legislation. However complete and exhaustive the listing may be there is always the possibility of some subject remaining unenumerated. Every Federation has to provide for such a contingency and lay down to whom the powers to legislate regarding these residuary subjects shall belong. Should they be given to the Central Government or should they be given to the Units ? Hitherto there has been only one way of dealing with them. In some Federations, these residuary powers are given to the Central Government, as in Canada. In some Federations they are given to the Units, as in Australia. The Indian Federation has adopted a new way of dealing with them. In the Indian Federation they are neither assigned to the Central Government nor to the Provinces. They are in a way vested in the Governor-General by virtue of Section 104. When a Legislation is proposed on a subject which is not enumerated in any of the three lists it is the Governor-General, who is to decide whether the powers shall be exercised by the Federal Legislature or by the Provincial Legislature.

(b) Executive Powers of the Federation.

The first question is, what is the extent of the executive powers of the Federation ? Is it co-extensive with the legislative powers ? In some of the Federations this was not made clear by statute. It was left to judicial decision. Such is the case in Canada. The Indian Constitution does not leave this matter to courts to decide. It is defined expressly in the Act itself. The relevant section is Section 8 (1). It says that the executive authority of the Federation extends :—

(a) to matters with respect to which the Federal Legislature has power to make laws.

(b) to raising in British India on behalf of His Majesty of naval, military and air forces and to the governance of His Majesty's forces borne on the Indian establishment.

(c) to the exercise of such rights, authority and jurisdiction as are exercisable by His Majesty by treaty, grant, usage, sufferance, or otherwise in and in relation to the tribal areas.

There is no difficulty in following the provisions of this Sub-section. There might perhaps be some difficulty in understanding sub-clause (a). It says that the executive power must be co-extensive with the legislative power of the Federation. Now the legislative power of the Federation extends not only to the Federal List but also to the Concurrent List. Does the executive power of the Federation extend to subjects included in the Concurrent List ? Two points must be borne in mind before answering this question. First, the Concurrent List is also subject to the legislative authority of the Province. Second, according to Section 49 (2) that the executive authority of each Province extends to the matters with respect to which the Legislature of the Province has power to make laws. The answer to the question whether the executive authority of the Federation extends also to Concurrent list is that the Executive Authority in respect of the Concurrent List belongs to the Federal Government as well as to the Provincial Government. This is clear from the terms of section 126 (2). It belongs to Provincial Government except in so far as the Federal Legislature has covered the field. It belongs to the Federal Government except in so far as the Provincial Legislature has covered the field.

The Concurrent List is not the only list which is subject to Legislation by the Federal Legislature. The Federal Legislature has the right to legislate even on Provincial subjects under section 102 in cases of emergency and under Section 106 to give effect to international agreements. Does the Executive Authority of the Federation extend to such matters also? The answer is that when a field is covered by Federal Legislation that field also becomes the field of Executive Authority of the Federation.

(c) Administrative Powers of the Federation.

The Administrative Powers of the Federation follow upon the Executive Powers of the Federation just as the Executive Powers of the Federation follow upon the Legislative Powers of the Federation.

To this there is one exception. That exception relates to the administration of subjects included in the Concurrent List. The Concurrent List is a list to which the Legislative Authority of the Federation extends by virtue of Section 100. As has already been pointed out the executive authority of the Federation extends in so far as Federal Legislation has covered the field. But the administrative powers for subjects falling in the Concurrent List do not belong to the Federation. They belong to the Provinces.

(b) Financial Powers of the Federation.

The revenues of the Federal Government are derived from four different sources: (1) Revenue from Commercial enterprises, (2) Revenue from Sovereign Functions; (3) Revenue from Tributes; and (4) Revenue from Taxes.

Under the first head fall all revenues from Posts and Telegraphs, Federal Railways, banking profits and other commercial operations. Under the second head come revenues from currency and coinage, from *bona vacantia* and territories administered directly by the Federal Government. Under the third head are included Contributions and Tributes from the Indian States.

The classification of Revenue from taxes follows upon the Powers of Taxation given to the Federal Government by the Constitution. The Powers of Taxation given to the Federal Government fall into three main categories. In the first category fall those powers of taxation which are exercisable for raising revenue which is wholly appropriable by the Federal Government. In the second category, fall those powers of taxation which are exercisable for raising revenue which is wholly appropriable by the Provincial Governments. In the third category fall those powers of taxation which are exercisable for raising revenue which is divisible between the Federal Government and the Provincial Governments.

The heads of revenue which fall under the first category of Taxing Powers cover those which are specifically mentioned in the Federal List.

1. Duties of customs, including export duties.

2. Duties of excise on tobacco and other goods manufactured or produced in India except.—

(a) alcoholic liquors for human consumption:

(b) opium, Indian hemp and other narcotic drugs and narcotics, non-narcotic drugs ;

(c) medical and toilet preparations containing alcohol, or any substance included in sub paragraph (b) of this entry.

3. Corporation tax.

4. Salt.

5. State lotteries.

6. Taxes on income other than agricultural income.

7. Taxes on the capital value of the assets, exclusive of agricultural land of individuals and companies ; taxes on the capital of companies.

8. Duties in respect of succession to property other than agricultural land.

9. The rates of stamp duty in respect of bills of exchange, cheques, promissory notes, bills of lading, letters of credit, policies of insurance, proxies and receipts.

10. Terminal taxes on goods or passengers carried by railway or air ; taxes on railway fares and freights.

11. Fees in respect of any of the matters in this list but not including fees taken in any court.

In connection with this, attention might be drawn to the following items in the Concurrent List:-

1. Marriage and divorce.

2. Wills, intestacy and succession.

3. Transfer of Property and other agricultural lands.

Being in the Concurrent list, the Federal Legislature has power to legislate upon with respect to these. Can the Federal Legislature also while legislating upon them raise revenue from them? The Act does not seem to furnish any answer to this question. It may however be suggested that the rules contained in Sec. 104 regarding the exercise of Residuary Powers will also apply here.

The sources of revenue which are ma de divisible by the Constitution are: (1) Income Tax other than Corporation Tax and (2) Jute Export duty. Those which are made divisable according to the Federal Law are (1) Duty on Salt, (2) Excise duty on Tobacco and other goods and (3) Duties of Export.

In respect of the financial powers of the Federation there is one feature which by reason of its peculiarity is deserving of attention. The Act, in giving the Federal Government the right to tax, makes a distinction between power to levy the tax and the right to collect it and even where it gives the power to levy the tax it does not give it the right to collect it. This is so in the case of surcharge on Income tax and the Corporation tax. The Income tax is only leviable in the Provinces and not in the States although it is a tax for Federal purposes. The State subjects are liable to pay only a Federal surcharge on Income Tax because such a surcharge is leviable both within the Provinces as well as the States. But under Sec. 138 (3) the Federal Government has no right to collect it within the States. The collection is left to the Ruler of the State. The Ruler, instead of collecting the surcharge from his subjects, may agree to pay the Federation a lump sum and the Federation is bound to accept the same. Similar is the case with regard to the Corporation tax. The Federation can levy it on state subjects but cannot collect it directly by its own agency. Section 139 provides that the collection of the Corporation tax shall as of right be the function of the Ruler.

V. CHARACTER OF THE FEDERATION.

(1) The nature of the Union

How does the Indian Federation compare with other Federations? This is not only a natural inquiry but it is also a necessary inquiry. The method of comparison and contrast is the best way to understand the nature of a thing. This comparison can be instituted from many points of view. There is no time for a comparison on so vast a scale. I must confine this comparison to some very moderate dimensions. Therefore I propose to raise only four questions: (1) Is this Federation a perpetual Union? (2) What is the relationship of the Units to the Federal Government? (3) What is the relationship of the Units as between themselves? (4) What is the relationship of the people under the Units?

There is no doubt that the accession of the Indian States to the Federation is to be perpetual so long as the Federation created by the Act is in existence. While the Federation exists there is no right to secede. But that is not the real question. The real question is, will the federation continue even when the Act is changed? In other words the question is, is this a perpetual Union with no right to secede or, is this a mere alliance with a right to break away? In my opinion the Indian Federation is not a perpetual union and that the Indian States have a right to secede. In this respect the constitution of the United States and this Indian Federation stand in clear contrast. The constitution of the United States says nothing as to the right of secession. This omission was interpreted in two different ways. Some said that it was not granted because it was copy recognized. Others said it was not excluded because it was not negatived. It was this controversy over the question namely whether the right of secession was excluded because it was not recognized which led to the Civil War of 1861. The Civil War settled two important principles : (1) No state has a right to declare an Act of the Federal Government invalid; (2) No State has a right to secede from the Union. In the Indian Federation it would be unnecessary to go to war for establishing the right to secession because the constitution recognizes the right of the Indian States to secede from the Indian Federation if certain eventualities occur. What is a perpetual Union and what is only a compact is made nowhere so clear as by Blackstone in his analysis of the nature of the Union between England and Scotland. To use his language the Indian Federation is not an incorporate Union because in a Union the two contracting States are totally annihilated without any power of revival. The Indian Federation is an alliance between two contracting parties, the Crown and the Indian States, in which neither is annihilated but each reserves a right to return to original status if a breach of condition occurs. The Constitution of the United States originated in a compact but resulted in a Union. The Indian Federation originates in a compact and continues as a compact. That the Indian Federation has none of the marks of a Union but on the other hand it has all the marks of a compact is beyond dispute. The distinguishing marks of a Union were well described by Daniel Webster, when in one of his speeches on the American Constitution he said :—

"...The constitution speaks of that political system which is established as 'the Government of the United States'. Is it not doing a strange violence to language to call a league or a compact between sovereign powers a *Government*? The Government of a State is that organization in which political power resides.

"...The broad and clear difference between a government and a league or a compact is that a government is a body politic; it has a will of its own; and it possesses powers and faculties to execute its own purposes. Every compact looks to some power to enforce its stipulations. Even in a compact between sovereign communities, there always exists this ultimate reference to a power to insure its execution; although, in such a case, this power is but the force of one party against the force of another; that is to say, the power of war. But a *Government* executes its decisions by its own supreme authority. Its use of force in compelling obedience to its own enactments is not war. It contemplates no opposing party having a right of resistance. It rests on its power to enforce its own will; and when it ceases to possess this power it is no longer a Government."

In the light of this the following facts should be noted. The Act does not ordain and establish a Federal Government for British India and the Indian States. The Act ordains and establishes a Federal Government for British India only. The Federal Government will become a Government for the States only when each State adopts it by its Instrument of Accession. Again note that the subjection of the States to the Federal Government is not to be for all times. It is to continue only under certain circumstances. It is to continue so long as certain provisions of the Act are continued without a change. Thirdly, where change in the provisions is permissible such change shall not bind the State unless it agrees to be bound by it.

All these are unmistakable signs which show that the Indian Federation is a compact and not a perpetual Union. The essence of a compact is that it reserves the right to break away and to return to the original position.

In this respect therefore the Indian Federation differs from the Federations in U. S. A., Canada, and Australia. It differs from the U.S.A., because the right to secede is recognized by the Indian Constitution if the constitution is altered, while it is not recognized by the Constitution of the U. S. A., even if the constitution is altered against the wishes of a particular State. In regard to Australia and Canada such a question cannot really arise and if it did, a civil war would be quite unnecessary to decide the issue. In these federations the sovereignty whether it is exercised by the Federal Governments or the Units belongs to the Crown and the maintenance of the Federation or its break up remains with the King and Parliament. Neither the Federation nor the Units could decide the issue otherwise than with the consent of Parliament. If a break up came, it would be a mere withdrawal of the sovereignity of the Crown and its re-distribution which the Crown is always free to do. The break up could be legal and even if it was perpetrated by non-legal means it could give sovereignty to the rebellious units because it belongs to the Crown. The same would have been the case, if the Indian Federation had been the Federation of British India Provinces only. No question of secession could have arisen. The Provinces would have been required to remain in the position in which the Crown might think it best to place them. The Indian Federation has become different because of the entry of the Indian States. The entry of the Indian States is not for all times and under all circumstances. Their entry is upon terms and conditions. That being so the Indian Federation could not be a perpetual union. Indeed, the Indian States would not enter into matrimony with the Indian Provinces unless the terms of divorce were settled before-hand. And so they are." That is why the Indian Federation is a compact and not a union.

(2) Relationship of the Units to the Federal Government.

That each separate unit should have approximately equal political rights is a general feature of federations. Equality of status among the different units is a necessity. To make them unequal in status is to give some units the power to become dominant partners. The existence of dominant partners in a federation, as observed by Dicey is fraught with two dangers. Firstly, the dominant partners may exercise an authority almost inconsistent with federal equality. Secondly, it may create combinations inside the Federation of dominant units and subordinate units and *vice versa*. To prevent such an unhealthy state of affairs, all federations proceed upon the principle of equality of status. How far does this principle obtain in the Indian Federation?

(a) In the matter of Legislation.

As you know for purposes of Legislation the field is divided into three parts and there are three lists prepared which are called the Federal List, the Concurrent List and the Provincial List.

The Federal List contains 59 items as subjects of legislation. The Concurrent List contains 36 items.

The first thing to note is that both these lists are binding upon the Provinces. They cannot escape them. They cannot pick and choose as to the matters in these two lists in respect of which they will subject themselves to the authority of the Federation. The Provinces have no liberty to contract out of these two lists. The position of a Federating State is quite different. A Federating State can wholly keep itself out of the Concurrent List. Under section 6 (2) there is no objection to the Ruler of any Indian State to agree to federate in respect of matters included in the Concurrent List. But there is no obligation upon them to do so. Such an agreement is not a condition precedent to their admission into the Federation.

With regard to the Federal List, there is no doubt an obligation on the Ruler of a State to subject himself to the legislative authority of the Federation in respect of the Federal List, but his subjection to the Federation will be confined to matters specified by him in his Instrument of

Accession. There are as I stated altogether 59 items in the Federal List. There is no obligation upon the Prince to accept all subjects in the Federal List as a condition precedent for his entry into Federation. He may accept some only or he may accept all. Again one Ruler may accept one item and another Ruler may accept another. There is no rule laid down in the constitution that some items must be accepted by every Ruler who chooses to enter the Federation. The Federation, therefore, while it affects British India and the Provinces uniformly and completely so far as the legislative authority of the Federation is concerned, it touches different States in different degrees. A Ruler may federate in respect of one subject yet he is as good a member of the Federation as a Ruler who accepts all the fiftynine items in the Federal List.

The Provincial List is a list which is subject to the exclusive Legislative authority of the Provinces. There is no corresponding State List given in the Act for the Federated States. It cannot be given. But it can be said that it includes all these subjects which are not surrendered by the State to the Federation. Now with regard to the Provincial List although it is subject to the exclusive authority of the Provincial Legislature, still in the event of emergency it is open to the Federal Legislature to make laws for a Province or any part thereof with respect to any of the matters enumerated in the Provincial List, if the Governor-General has in his discretion declared under Section 102 by proclamation that a grave emergency exists whereby the security of India is threatened whether by way of war or by internal disturbances. There is no such provision in respect of the Indian States. A grave emergency which threatens India may quite well arise within a State as it may within the territories of a Province. It is thus clear that while the Federal Legislature can intervene and make laws for a Province when there is emergency, it cannot intervene and make laws for the Federated States under similar circumstances.

(2) In the matter of the Executive.

Again in the matter of the Executive, the States and the Provinces do not stand on the same footing. Section 8 defines the scope of the executive authority of the Federation which according to Section 7 is exercisable by the Governor-General on behalf of His Majesty. According to sub-section (1) to sub-clause (a) the authority of the Federal Executive extends to matters with respect to which the Federal Legislature has power to make laws, but this clause has not the same application with respect to the States as it has with respect to the provinces. With regard to the provinces it has authority in all matters which are included in the

Federal Legislative List. It has also exclusive authority with respect to certain matters included in the Concurrent List subject to certain limitations; but with regard to the States the case is very different. With regard to the States the Federation can have no executive authority in respect of subjects in the Concurrent List, but also the Federation is not entitled to have exclusive authority with respect to matters included in the Federal Legislative List. Sub-Clause 2 of Section 8 is very important. It says :—

"The executive authority of the ruler of a Federated State shall, notwithstanding anything in this section, continue to be exercisable in that State with respect to matters with respect to which the Federal Legislature has power to make laws for that State except in so far as the executive authority of the Federation becomes exercisable in the State to the exclusion of the executive authority of the Ruler by virtue of a federal law."

In plain language what the sub-section means is this. With regard to a province the executive authority of the Federation extends to all matters over which the Federation has legislative authority. With regard to the State the position is different. The mere fact that the federal legislature has authority to legislate in respect of a subject does not give the Federation any executive authority over the State in respect of that subject. Such executive authority can be conferred only as a result of a law passed by the Federation. Whether it is possible to pass such a law is problematic in view of the large representation which the States have in Federal Legislature. Whatever may be the eventuality, in theory the executive authority of the Federation does not extend to a Federated State. The position is that while with regard to the provinces the Federation can legislate as well as execute, in the case of the Federated States, the Federation can legislate, but cannot execute. The execution may be with the State.

In the matter of administration.

When you begin to examine the constitution from the point of view of administration you will find certain sections in the Act which lay down rules for the guidance of the Federal Government, of the Provincial Governments and of the State Governments. The purpose of the sections is to tell them how they should exercise the executive authority belonging to them respectively. These sections are 122, 126 and 128.

Section 122 is addressed to the Federal Government. It reads as follows :—

"122. (1) The executive authority of every Province and Federated State shall be so exercised as to secure respect for the laws of the Federal Legislature which apply in that Province or State.

(2) The reference in sub-section (1) of this Section to laws of the Federal Legislature shall, in relation to any Province, include a reference to any existing Indian Law applying in that Province.

(3) Without prejudice to any of the other provisions of this part of this Act, in the exercise of the excutive authority of the Federation in any Province or Federated State regard shall be had to the interests of that Province or State.

Section 126 is addressed to the Provincial Governments. It provides that :—

> "126.—(1) The executive authority of every Province shall be so exercised as not to impede or prejudice the exercise of the executive authority of the Federation, and the executive authority of the Federation shall extend to the giving of such directions to a Province as may appear to the Federal Government to be necessary for that purpose."

Section 128 is addressed to the States. It runs as follows :—

> "128.—(1) The executive authority of every Federated State shall be so exercised as not to impede or prejudice the exercise of the executive authority of the Federation so far as it is exercisable in the State by virtue of a law

of the Federal Legislature which applies therein.

(2) If it appears to the Governor-General that the Ruler of any Federated State has in any way failed to fulfil his obligations under the preceding sub-section, the Governor-General, acting in his discretion, may after considering any representations made to him by the Ruler, issue such directions to the Ruler as he thinks fit:—

Provided that, if any question arises under this section as to whether the executive authority of the Federation is exercisable in a State with respect to any matter or as to the extent to which it is so exercisable, the question may, at the instance either of the Federation or the Ruler, be referred to the Federal Court for determination by that Court in the exercise of its original jurisdiction under this Act".

All these sections would have been very useful if there was any possibility of conflict in the exercise of their executive authority by these agencies. But these will be quite unnecessary because there would be as a matter of fact no conflict of executive authority which can arise only when such executive authority is followed by administrative act. When administration is divorced from Executive Authority there is no possibility of conflict and the admonitions contained in such sections are quite unnecessary.

Now it is possible that in the Federal Constitution the Federal Government may be altogether denuded of its powers of administration and may be made just as a frame without any spring of action in it. The constitution provides that the Governor-General or the Federal Legislature may provide that the administration of a certain law passed by it instead of being carried on by the Federal Executive might be entrusted to the Units i.e. to the Provincial Governments and the Indian States. This is clear from the terms of section 124 :—

> " 124.—(1) Notwithstanding anything in this Act, the Governor-General may, with the consent of the Government of a Province or the Ruler of a Federated State, entrust either conditionally to the Government or Ruler, or to their respective officers, functions in relation to any matter to which the executive authority of the Federation extends.
>
> (2) An Act of the Federal Legislature may, notwithstanding that it relates to a matter with respect to which a Provincial Legistature has no power to make laws, confer powers and impose duties upon a Province or officers and authorities thereof.

(3) An Act of the Federal Legislature which extends to a Federated State may confer powers and impose duties upon the State or officers and authorities thereof to be designated for the purpose by the Ruler.

(4) Where by virtue of this section powers and duties have been conferred or imposed upon a Province or a Federated State or officers or authorities thereof, there shall be paid by the Federation to the Province or State such sum as may be agreed, or, in default of agreement, as may be determined by an arbitrator appointed by the Chief Justice of India, in respect of any extra costs of administration incurred by the Province or State in connection with the exercise of those powers and duties."

It is quite possible for States and Provinces to combine to rob the Federation of all administrative powers and make it only a law making body.

A more staggering situation however is created by Section 125. It is in the following terms :—

"125.—(1) Notwithstanding anything in this Act, agreements may, and, if provision has been made in that behalf by the Instrument of Accession of the State, shall be made between the Governor-

General and the Ruler of a Federated State for the exercise by the Ruler or his officers of functions in relation to the administration in his State of any law of the Federal Legislature which applies therein..

(2) An agreement made under this section shall contain provisions enabling the, Governor-General in his discretion to satisfy himself, by inspection or otherwise that the administration of the law to which the agreement relates is carried out in accordance with the policy of the Federal Government and, if he is not so satisfied, the Governor-General, acting in his discretion, may issue such directions to the Ruler as he thinks fit.

(3) All courts shall take judicial notice of any agreement made under this section."

This section means that a State by its Instrument of Accession may stipulate that the administration of Federal laws in the State shall be carried out by the State agency and not by the agency of the Federation and if it does so stipulate then the Federation shall have no administrative power inside the State. The benefit of a law depends upon its administration. A law may turn out to be of no avail because the administration is either inefficient or corrupt. To deprive the Federal Government of its administrative powers is really to cripple the Federal Government. There is no Federation in which some units of the Federation are permitted to say that the Federal Government shall have no administrative powers in their territory. The Indian Federation is an exception. Not only is there a difference between the Provinces and the States in this matter but they also differ in their liability to supervision and direction by the Federal Government in the matter of the exercise of their executive authority. That difference will be clear if you will compare Section 126 with Section 128.

Section 126 enacts that the executive authority of every province shall be so exercised as not to impede or prejudice the exercise of the executive authority of the Federation and the executive authority of the Federation shall extend to the giving of such directions to a Province as may appear to the Federal Government to be necessary for that purpose. Section 128 is a section which enacts a similar rule with respect to a Federated State, but there is a significant difference between the two sections. Section 126 says that the executive authority of the Federation extends to the giving of such directions to a province as may appear to the Federal Government to be necessary for that purpose, while Section 128 does not give such a power. That means that the Federation does not possess the inherent executive authority to give a direction to the Ruler of a Federated State to prevent him from so exercising the executive authority of the State as to impede or prejudice the exercise of the executive authority of the Federation. That is one very significant difference. Such authority, instead of being given to the Federation, is given to the Governor-General, who, of course, under the law is distinct from the Federal Government and it is the Governor-General who is empowered to issue such directions to the Ruler as he thinks fit. A further distinction is also noticeable. When directions are issued to the Governor of a province under Section 126 he is bound to carry them out. He has no right to question the necessity of the directions nor can he question the capacity of the Governor-General to issue such directions. With regard to the Ruler of a State, however, the position is entirely different. He can question such a direction, and have the matter adjudicated in the Federal Court, because the proviso to sub-section 2 of Section 128 says that if any question arises under this section as to whether the executive authority under this section of the Federation is exercisable in a State with respect to any matter or as to the extent to which it is so exercisable, the question may at the instance either of the Federation or the Ruler be referred to the Federal Court for determination by that Court.

(d) In the matter of Finance.

Coming to the question of Finance, the disparity between the Provinces and the States is a glaring disparity. Take the case of the taxing authority of the Federation over the Provinces and the States. It may be noted that the revenues of the Federation are derivable from sources which fall under two main heads : Those derived from taxation and those not derived from taxation. Those not derived from taxation fall under six heads :—

(1) Fees in respect of matters included in the Federal List.

(2) Profits, if any, on the work of the Postal Services, including Postal Savings Banks.

(3) Profits, if any, on the operation of Federal Railways.

(4) Profits, if any, from Mint and Currency operations.

(5) Profits, if any, from any other Federal enterprise, such as Reserve Bank, and

(6) Direct contribution to the Crown from Federated or non-Federated States.

As regards the revenues derived from taxation under the Government of India Act, they fall under two heads ; Ordinary taxation and Extraordinary taxation. Ordinary taxation includes levy from following sources :—

(1) Customs duties.
(2) Export duties.
(3) Excise duties.
(4) Salt.
(5) Corporation tax.
(6) Tax on income, other than agricultural, and
(7) Property Taxes i. e., taxes on Capital value of the individual assets or a property.

The extraordinary revenue falls under following heads :—

(1) Surcharges on Income tax.
(2) „ on succession duties.
(3) „ on terminal taxes on goods or passengers carried by rail or air and all taxes on railway freights
(4) Surcharges on Stamp duties, etc.

Now, while the provinces are liable to bear taxation under any of these heads whether the taxation is of an ordinary character or is of an extra-ordinary character, the same is not true of the States. For instance, the States are not liable in ordinary times to ordinary taxes falling under heads 6 and 7, while the Provinces are liable.

With regard to extraordinary taxation, the States are not liable to contribute even in times of financial stringency the taxes levied under items

2, 3 and 4 and even where they are liable to contribute under head 1 of the extra-ordinary sources of revenue, it must be certified that all other economies have been made.

There is another difference from the financial point of view between the States and the Provinces. The field of taxation for provincial governments has been defined in the Act. A provincial government cannot raise revenue from any source other than those mentioned in the Act. Such is not the case with the State. There is nothing in the Government of India Act, which defines the powers of a Federated State with regard to its system of taxation. It may select any source of taxation to raise revenue for the purpose of internal administration and may even levy customs duties upon articles entering its territory from a neighbouring province, although that neighbouring province is a unit of the Federal Government of which the Federated State is also a unit." This is a most extra-ordinary feature of this Indian Federation and also one of its worst features. One of the results of a Federation, if not its primary object, has been the freedom of trade and commerce inside the territory of the Federation." There is no federation known to history which has permitted one unit of the Federation to levy customs duties or raise other barriers with a view to prevent inter-state commerce. The Indian Federation is an exception to that rule and this is a feature of the

Indian Federation which makes it stand out in glaring contrast with other federations with which people are familiar today.

One of the characteristics of a Federal Constitution is that although the territory comprised in the Federation is distributed or held by different units, still they constitute one single territory. At any rate for customs purposes the territory is treated as a single unit. Every Federal Constitution contains powers and prohibitions to prevent trade and customs barriers being erected by one unit against another.

The American constitution by Section 9 of Article II prohibits a state from preventing the import or export of goods or from levying import or export duties upon goods passing in or out of the state boundary. Section 8 (3) of Article II gives the Federal Government the power of regulating trade or commerce between the states of the Union.

In Australia by virtue of Section 92 of its constitution both the States and the Federal Government are bound so to exercise their power of regulation as not to transgress the fundamental guarantee of the constitution embodied in Section 92 that "trade and commerce among the states whether by means of internal carriage or ocean navigation shall be absolutely free."

In Canada Section 121 enacts that "all articles of the growth, produce or manufacture of any one

Province shall, from and after the Union, be admitted free into each of the other Provinces."

In the Indian Constitution the provision relating to freedom of trade and commerce within the Federation is contained in Section 297. It reads as follows :—

"297 (1) No Provincial Legislature or Government shall :—

(a) by virtue of the entry in the Provincial Legislative List relating to trade and commerce within the Province, or the entry in that list relating to the production, supply, and distribution of commodities, have power to pass any law or take any executive action prohibiting or restricting the entry into, or export from, the Province of goods of any class or description ; or

(b) by virtue of anything in this Act have power to impose any tax, cess, toll, or due which, as between goods manufactured or produced in the Province and similar goods not so manufactured or produced, discriminates in favour of the former, or which, in the case of goods manufactured or produced outside the Province, discriminates between goods manufactured or produced in one locality and similar goods manufactured or produced in another locality.

(2) Any law passed in contravention of this section shall, to the extent of the contravention, be invalid."

Now it will be clear from the terms of this section that the freedom of trade and commerce is confined only to the Provinces. That means the Indian States are free to prohibit the entry of goods from the Provinces absolutely or subject them to duty. This is quite contrary to the fundamental idea underlying a federal union. To allow one unit of the Federation to carry on commercial warfare against another unit is nothing but negation of federation.

(4) Relationship of the People under the Federation

Before I enter into this question it is necessary to clear the ground by pointing out certain distinctions. The words 'state' and 'society' are often presented as though there was a contrast between the two. But really there is no distinction of a fundamental character between a state and a society. It is true that the plenary powers of the state operate through the sanction of law while society depends upon religious and social sanctions for the enforcement of its plenary powers. The fact, however, remains that both have plenary powers to coerce. As such, there is no contrast between state and society. Secondly, the persons composing society are persons who are also members of the state. Here again, there is no difference between state and society.

There is, however, one difference, but it is of another kind. Every person, who is a member of society and dwells in it, is not necessarily a member of the state. Only those who belong to the state are members of the state. All those who dwell within the boundary of the state do not necessarily belong to the state. This distinction between those, who belong to the state and those who do not, is very crucial and should not be forgotten because it has important consequences. Those who belong to a state are members and have the benefits of membership which consists of the totality of rights and duties which they possess over against the State. From the side of duty the relation is best indicated by the word subject, from the side of rights it is best designated by the word citizen. This difference involves the consequence that those who dwell in the State without belonging to it have no benefit of membership which means that they are foreigners and not citizens.

Theoretically, the task of differentiating the foreigners from the citizens of a State would seem to be an easy task, in fact, almost a mechanical task. This is particularly true of an Unitary State. Here there is a simple question : What is the relation of this person to this State as against any and all foreign States ? In a Federal State the matter is complicated by the fact that every individual stands in a dual relationship. On the one hand, he sustains certain relations to the Federal state as a whole; and on the other he sustains certain relations to the state in which he may reside. The moment an attempt is made to define the status of a person in a Federal State, therefore, not one question, but several must be answered: What is the relation of this person to the Federal State, as against any and all foreign States? What is the relation of this person to the State in which he resides? Further is it possible to be a citizen of one state and not a citizen of the Federal State?

Such questions did not arise in Canada and Australia when they became federations. The reason was that persons residing in their respective units were natural born British subjects—a status which remained with them when the Federation came. After the Federation the power of naturalization was given to the Federation and consequently every one who is. naturalized by the Federation is a citizen of the federation and therefore of every unit in it.

Such questions however did arise in the U.S.A., Switzerland and Germany, because before the Federation their units were all foreign states and their subjects were foreign subjects. But it is noteworthy that in all these cases a common citizenship was established as a part of the federation. A rule was established whereby it was accepted that a citizenship of one unit carried with it a citizenship of the Federation.

The case of the Indian Federation is similar to that of the U.S.A., Germany and Switzerland. The subject of an Indian State is a foreigner in British India as well as in another Indian State. The subject of a British Indian Province is a foreigner in every Indian State.

What does the Indian Federation do with regard to this matter? Does it forge a common Citizenship for all Units which become members of the Federation? The answer is no. A British Indian will continue to be a foreigner in every Indian State even though it is a Federated State after the Federation, as he was before the Federation. Similarly a subject of a Federated Indian State will be a foreigner in every British Indian Province after the federation as he was before Federation. There is no common nationality. The whole principle of the Federation is that the ruler of a Federated State shall remain the ruler of the state and his subjects shall remain his subjects and the Crown as the ruler of the Federated Provinces shall remain the ruler of the Provinces and his subjects shall remain his subjects.

This difference in citizenship manifests itself in two specific ways.

Firstly, it manifests itself in the matter of right to serve. Federation being established under the

Crown, only persons who are subjects of the Crown are entitled to serve under it. This is recognized by Section 262. This of course is an injustice to the subjects of the States. To prevent this injustice which of course is a logical consequence of difference of citizenship, power is given to the Secretary of State to declare the subjects of the Indian States eligible for service under the Federation. This is an anomalous state of affairs and although the injustice to Indian State subjects is mitigated, the injustice against British Indians in the matter of right to employment in Indian States continues. For, Indian States are not required to declare that British Indians shall be deemed to be eligible for service under them. That notwithstanding federation such an anomaly should exist shows that this Federation is a freak.

Secondly, this difference in citizenship shows itself in the terms of the oath prescribed for members of the Legislature by Schedule IV.

In the case of a member who is a British subject the form of the oath is as under:—

> "I, A. B., having been elected (or nominated or appointed) a member of this Council (or Assembly), do solemnly swear (or affirm) that I will be faithful and bear true allegiance to His Majesty the King, Emperor of India, His heirs and successors, and that I will faithfully discharge

> the duty upon which I am about to enter."

In the case of a person who is a subject of a Ruler of an Indian State the form of the oath is as follows :—

> " I, A. B., having been elected (or nominated or appointed) a member of this Council (or Assembly), do solemnly swear (or affirm) that saving the faith and allegiance which I owe to C. D., his heirs and successors, I will be faithful and bear true allegiance in my capacity as Member of this Council (or Assembly) to His Majesty the King, Emperor of India, His heirs and successors, and that I will faithfully discharge the duty upon which I am about to enter."

The subject of an Indian State, it is obvious from the terms of the oath, owes a double allegiance. He owes allegiance to the ruler of his State and also to the King. Superficially the position seems not very different from what one finds in the United States. In the United States the individual is a citizen of the Union as well as of the State and owes allegiance to both powers. Each power has a right to command his obedience. But ask the question, to which, in case of conflict, is obedience due and you will see the difference between the two. On this question this is what Bryce has to say :—

"The right of the State to obedience is wider in the area of matters which it covers. Prima Facie, every State-law, every order of a competent State authority binds the citizen, whereas the National government has but a limited power; it can legislate or command only for certain purposes or on certain subjects. But within the limits of its power, its authority is higher than that of the State, must be obeyed even at the risk of disobeying the State."

" Any act of a State-legislature or a State-executive conflicting with the Constitution, or with an act of the National government, done under the Constitution, is really an act not of the State-government, which cannot legally act against the Constitution, but of persons falsely assuming to act as such government, and is therefore ipso jure void. Those who disobey Federal authority on the ground of the commands of a State authority are therefore insurgents against the Union who must be coerced by its power. The coercion of such insurgents is directed not against the State but against them as individuals though combined wrongdoers. A State cannot secede and cannot rebel. Similarly, it cannot be coerced."

Can the Federal Government in India take the stand which the Union Government can when there is a conflict of allegiance ? There can be no doubt that it cannot, for the simple reason that the allegiance to the King saves the allegiance to the Ruler. This is a very unhappy if not a dangerous situation.

(5) Strength of the Federal Frame

The existence in the country of one Government which can speak and act in the name of and with the unified will of the whole nation is no doubt the strongest Government that can be had and only a strong Government can be depended upon to act in an emergency. The efficiency of a Governmental system must be very weak where there exists within a country a number of Governments which are distinct centres of force, which constitute separately organized political bodies into which different parts of the nation's strength flows and whose resistance to the will of the Central Government is likely to be more effective than could be the resistance of individuals, because such bodies are each of them endowed with a government, a revenue, a militia, a local patriotism to unite them. The former is the case where the unitary system of Government prevails. The latter is the case where the Federal form of Government prevails.

The Indian Federation by reason of the fact hat it is a Federation has all the weaknesses of a Federal form of Government. But the Indian Federation has its own added weaknesses which are not to be found in other Federations and which are likely to devitalize it altogether· Compare the Indian Federation with the Federation of the United States. As Bryce says "the authority of the national Government over the citizens of every State is direct and immediate, not exerted through the State organization, and not requiring the co-operation of the State Government. For most purposes the National Government ignores the States, and it treats the citizens of different States as being simply its own citizens, equally bound by its laws. The Federal Courts, Revenue Officers and Post Office draw no help from any State Officials, but depend directly on Washington..................There is no local self-Government in Federal matters..................The Federal authority, be it executive or judicial, acts upon the citizens of a State directly by means of its own officers who are quite distinct from and independent of State Officials. Federal indirect taxes, for instance, are levied all along the coast and over the country by Federal custom-house collectors and excisemen, acting under the orders of the treasury department at Washington. The judgments of Federal Courts are carried out by U. S. Marshals, likewise dispersed over the country and supplied with a staff of assistants. This is a provision of the utmost importance, for it enables the central, national Government to keep its fingers upon the people everywhere, and make its laws and the commands of its duly constituted authorities respected whether the State within whose territory it acts be heartily loyal or not, and whether the law which is being enforced be popular or obnoxious. The machinery of the national Government ramifies over the whole union as the nerves do over the whole body, placing every point in direct connection with the central executive."

Not one of these things can be predicated of the Indian Federation. It is a dependent Government and its relation with the people is not direct.

In the United States, the States, as States have no place in the Central Government and although the States elect representatives to the Federal Legislature, political action at the centre does not run in State channels. There is no combination of States into groups and it is not the fashion for States to combine in an official way through their State organizations. How different is the Indian Federation ! States, as such, have been given *de jure* recognition, they have been given *de jure* exemptions, and immunities from law. There are great possibilities of combined action and counteraction by States and Provinces over these exemptions and immunities. This is another reason which leads to the feeling that the Indian Federation will have very little vitality.

(6) Benefits of the Federal Scheme.

The protagonists of the Federal Scheme have urged three grounds in favour of the acceptance of the Scheme. The first ground is that it helps to unite India. The second ground is that it enables British India to influence Indian India and to gradually transform the autocracy that is prevalent in Indian India into the democracy that exists in British India. The third ground is that the Federal Scheme is a scheme which embodies what is called Responsible Government.

These three arguments in favour of the Federal Scheme are urged in such seriousness and the authority of those who urge them is so high that it becomes necessary to examine the substance that underlies them.

1. Federation and the Unity of India.

The advantages of common system of Government are indeed very real. To have a common system of law, a common system of administration and a feeling of oneness are some of the essentials of good life. But they are all the results which follow from a common life led under a common system of Government. Other things being equal, a federation as a common system of Government for the whole of India should be welcome. But does this Federation unite under one governmental system the whole territory called India in the Government of India Act 1935? Is this an All India Federation?

That this federation includes British India is of course true ; when Provinces are declared to be the units of the Federation it means that British India is included in the Federation. Because the Provinces which are declared to be the units of the Federation comprise what is called British India. There remains the question of the Indian States or what is called Indian India. Indian India is no small tract. The following figures of area and population will give a comparative idea of the extent of British India and this Indian India.

	Area in square Miles (1931).	Population. (1931)
British India excluding Burma and Aden. ...	8,62,630	2,56,859,787
Indian States. ...	7,12,508	81,310,845

It will be seen that Indian India comprises 39 p. c. of the population and 31 per cent of India as a whole.

How much of this Indian India is going to be brought under this Federation ?

Many will be inclined to say that as this is spoken of as an All India Federation every inch of this area will be included in the Federation and will be subject to the authority of the Federal Government. Such an impression is no doubt created by the wording of Section 6 (1) which relates to the accession of the states. This section speaks of a Ruler declaring his desire to join the Federation and thereby suggesting that every State is entitled to join the Federation. If this is true, then no doubt the Federation can in course of time be an All India federation. But this impression is wrong. Such an impression cannot arise if section 6 (1) is read with Schedule I of the Act. Schedule I is merely thought of as a schedule which contains a Table of Seats for the Rulers. This is a very incomplete reading of the Schedule. The Schedule does more than that. It not only gives a table of seats, but also enumerates the States which are entitled to join the Federation and thereby fixes the maximum number of states which can come within the federation if they wish to do so. In other words it is not open to every state to join the Federation. Only those enumerated can join. This is the significance of the Table of Seats given in Schedule I.

What is the total number of the states which can join the Federation? Schedule I limits the number to 147. A number of questions crop up by reason of this limit fixed by the Schedule. According to official figures there are in all 627 States in India. That means 480 States will remain outside the Federation and can never become part of the Federation. Can this be called an All India Federation? If it is to be an All India Federation, why are these States excluded? What is the position of these excluded States? If they are States with sovereignty, why are they not allowed to join the Federation? If they are not states with sovereignty and if the sovereignty is with the Crown, why has the Crown not transferred its sovereignty to the Federation in respect of these territories? What will be the ultimate destiny of such excluded States? Will these be merged in some Indian States or will these be merged in some Indian Provinces? I mention all this, firstly because I want to show that this Federation is not an All India Federation and secondly because I want to draw attention to the move of some Indian States to get these excluded States to merge into them.

A second question may be raised. Will this Federation help to unite the people of British India and the Indian States into one nation?

A federation is necessarily a composite body. Within it are units which are smaller political communities. Above the units is a larger political community called the Federation. Whether these different political communities will remain merely political associations or whether they will develop a common social fabric leading ultimately to the formation of a nation will depend upon what form their association takes. As Bryce points out:—

"When within a large political community smaller communities are found existing, the relation of the smaller to the larger usually appears in one or other of the two following forms. One form is that of the League, in which a number of political bodies, be they monarchies or republics, are bound together so as to constitute for certain purposes, and especially for the purpose of common defence, a single body. The members of such a composite body or league are not individual men but communities. It exists only as an aggregate of communities, and will therefore vanish so soon as the communities which compose it separate themselves from one another. Moreover it deals with and acts upon these communities only. With the individual citizen it has nothing to do, no right of taxing him, or judging him, or making laws for him, for in all these matters it is to his own community that his allegiance is due.

" In the second form, the smaller communities are mere subdivisions of that greater one which we call a nation. They have been created, or at any rate they exist, for administrative purposes only. Such powers as they possess are powers delegated by the nation, and can be overridden by its will. The nation acts directly by its own officers, not merely on the communities, but upon every single citizen ; and the nation, because it is independent of these communities, would continue to exist were they all to disappear......"

The former is the case where the form of Government is a confederation. The latter is the case where there exists a unitary form of Government. A Federal Government is between the two. It must not however be assumed that nationalism is compatible only with a Unitary Government and incompatible with a Federal form of Government. It must be borne in mind that as a nation may be found in being, so also a nation may be brought into being. In a Federal Government there may be at the start no nation, it may be a collection of heterogeneous communities. But it is possible to have in the end a nation even under a Federal Government. The most striking case is that of the United States of America. Mr. Bryce relates a story which is both interesting as well as instructive. This is the story and I give it in his own words. "Some years ago the American Protestant Episcopal Church was occupied at its triennial Convention in revising its liturgy. It was thought desirable to introduce among the short sentence prayers a prayer for the whole people ; and an eminent New England Divine proposed the words 'O Lord, bless our nation'. Accepted one afternoon on the spur of the moment, the sentence was brought up next day for reconsideration, when so many objections were raised by the laity to the word 'nation', as importing too definite a recognition of national unity, that it was dropped, and instead there were adopted the words, 'O Lord, bless these United States.' Notwithstanding this prayer to the Lord, notwithstanding the reluctance to encourage the idea of a nation over against the idea of the states and notwithstanding the federal form of Government the United States is a nation. That it is a nation in the social sense of the word is incontrovertible."

How has this happened in the United States? Can we hope to see this happen in India under the Federal Scheme ? Bryce explains how this happened in America. He points out that in America "The Central or National Government is not a mere league, for it does not wholly depend on the component Communities which we call the States. It is itself a Commonwealth as well as a Union of Commonwealths, because it claims directly the obedience of every citizen, and acts immediately upon him through its Courts and executive officers". It can tax him, make law for him and judge him. In short it is the process of Government which is responsible largely if not wholly for moulding the Americans into a nation and that this was possible because in the Federal Form of Government of the United States there is a direct contact between the National Government and the individual.

Is this possible under the Indian Federal Scheme ? My answer is that such a thing is not possible. The people in the Indian States remain the subjects of the State. The Federal Government cannot deal with them directly.

Everything has to be done through the State. There is no contact between the two, not even for purposes of taxation. How can a feeling that they belong to the National Government grow in the subjects of the Indian States if they are excluded from any and every influence and are not even made to feel the existence of the National Government? I am afraid this United States of India will not be more than a mere body of United States. It has no potentiality of forging a nation out of these States and probably the framers of the Scheme have had no such intention at all.

(2) Democratization of Autocracies.

The other advantage of the Federal Scheme which is claimed by its protagonists is that it brings beneath the dome of a single political edifice the new democracies of British India and the ancient autocracies of the Indian States and that by bringing the two under one edifice it provides contact between democracy and autocracy and thus enables the democracy in British India to democratize the autocracies in the Indian States. To examine this argument and to see how much force there is behind it, it is well to note that the Indian States and the British Indian Provinces are geographically contiguous. There is regular intercourse between them. The people of British India and those of the Indian States racially, linguistically and culturally form parts of one whole. With all these contacts and with all the unity of race, religion, language and culture British India has not been able to influence at all the forms of government which are prevalent in the Indian States. On the contrary while British India has advanced from autocracy to democracy the Indian States have remained what they were with their fixed form of government. Unless therefore there is something special in the Act itself which enables British India to exercise its influence on the Indian States through the legislature and through the executive, this argument can have no substance at all. Is there anything in the Act which gives British India power to influence the States? In this connection reference may be made to Section 34 (1) which deals with the procedure in the legislature with respect to the discussion and voting of the Budgest estimates.

From an examination of this Section it will be clear that the estimates relating to para (a) and para (f) of sub-section (3) of Section 33 cannot even be discussed by the Federal legislature. Para (a) of Sub-section (3) refers to the salary and allowances of the Governor-General and other expenditure relating to his office for which estimate is required to be made by Orders in Council, and para (f) relates to the sums payable to His Majesty under this Act out of the revenue of the Federation in respect of the expenses incurred in discharging the functions of the Crown in its relations with the Indian States. Another section which has a bearing upon this point is Section 38. Section 38 is a section which deals with the making of the rules by the Federal legislature for regulating its procedure in the conduct of its business. While this section permits the Federal legislature to make its own rules it allows the Governor-General to make rules:

(c) For prohibiting the discussion of, or the asking of questions on, any matter connected with any Indian State, other than a matter with respect to which the Federal legislature has power to make laws for that State, unless the Governor-General in his discretion is satisfied that the matter affects Federal interest or affects a British subject, and has given his consent to the matter being discussed or the question being asked;

(d) For prohibiting:

(i) the discussion of, or the asking of questions on, any matter connected with relations between His Majesty or the Governor-General and any foreign State or Prince; or

(ii) the discussion, except in relation to estimates of expenditure of, or the asking of questions on, any matter connected with the tribal area or the the administration of any excluded area; or

(iii) the discussion of, or the asking of questions on, the personal conduct of the ruler of any Indian State, or of a member of the ruling family thereof ;

and the section further provides that if and so far as any rule so made by the Governor-General is inconsistent with any rules made by the Chamber, the rules made by the Governor-General shall prevail.

Another section having a bearing on this point is Section 40. It says: "No discussion shall take place in the Federal legislature with respect to the conduct of any judge of the Federal Court or a High Court in the discharge of his duties and provides that in this sub-section the reference to a High Court shall be construed as including a reference to any court in a Federated State which is a High Court for any of the purposes of Part 9 of this Act." Similar provisions are contained in that part of the Act which relates to the constitution of the provincial legislatures. Section 84 is a counterpart of Section 38 and prevents any member of a Provincial legislature from asking any question with regard to the personal conduct of the ruler of any Indian State or the affairs of a State. Section 86 is a counterpart of Section 40.

Now it is obvious that the two most important ways open to a Legislature for influencing the conduct of the administration is by discussion of the Budget and by asking questions. The discussion on the budget had its origin in the theory which postulates that there can be no supply given to the executive unless the grievances of the people were redressed. The slogan of democracy has been : Redress of grievances before supplies of moneys. The discussion on the budget is the one opportunity of placing the grievances of a people before the executive. It is therefore a very valid privilege, but as will be seen from Section 34 the legislature is prevented from placing the grievances of the subjects of the States before the executive on the floor of the House. Similarly, the right to interrogate and ask questions is also a valid privilege, but that also is denied. The right to criticise on a proper motion the conduct of the judiciary is always open to the legislature, but that also has been excluded. It is difficult to see exactly in what way the Federal legislature could influence the internal administration of the Indian States. Not only the representatives of British India are prevented from asking any question or moving any resolution with regard to the internal administration of the States, but the same disability is imposed upon the representatives of the States themselves who are the victims of this maladministration

Compare with this the influence which the Federated States are in a position to exercise over British India.

In the first place there is no restriction on the representatives of the Federated States in the matter of asking any question or raising any matter in the Federal Legislature. The fact that the question or matter touches British India and relates to internal administration of British India is not a bar against the representatives of the Federated States from raising such an issue.

Secondly, there is no restraint upon the representatives of the Federated States in the matter of discussing and voting upon the financial proposals of the Federal Government. The fact that any such proposal affects British India only and does not affect the States can cause no legal impediment in their way.

Thirdly, in the matter of Legislation the Representatives of the Federated States are free to vote upon any measure brought before the Federal Legislature. There are two lists over which the legislative authority of the Federation extends:—The Federal list and the Concurrent list. The provinces are wholly bound by the Federal List. A Federated State is not wholly bound by it. The provinces are wholly bound by the concurrent list. A Federated State may not be bound at all. Yet the State representatives have a right to vote upon any measure falling under either of the two lists. In other words the Federal Scheme gives the States the right to legislate for British India, while British India gets no such right to legislate for the States except to the extent to which the States choose to subject themselves to these two legislative lists.

The scope of this Legislative influence by the States over British India is by no means small nor is it inconsequential. To Confine to the Concurrent list only, it includes 36 subjects. Among the 36 are such subjects as, Criminal Law, Criminal and Civil Procedure, Professions, Newspapers, books and printing Press etc. It is clear that these subjects are vital subjects. They affect the liberties of the people in the Provinces. Now as the States have a right to participate and vote upon all legislation within the Concurrent list, the Indian States will have the right and the authority to pass legislation affecting the rights, privileges and liberties of British Indians in the Provinces.

Further in the Legislative sphere, so far as it relates to the Concurrent List the States have obtained authority without any obligation. They are free to legislate and need not consider their own case in doing so because they are not bound by the laws they make. Their conduct can be as irresponsible as they may choose to make it.

It is however an understatement to say that the States have only a right to influence administration and Legislation in British India. The truth is that the States can dominate British India because they can maintain in office a ministry in the Federal Government although it is defeated by a majority of the representatives of British India on a matter purely affecting British India. This is because they have a right to vote upon any motion including a non-confidence motion irrespective of the question whether the motion relates to a matter which affects them or not. If this does not vest control over British India in Indian States I wonder what will.

The injustice and anomaly of the States taking part in the discussions on the internal affairs of British India while the representatives of British India having no corresponding right to discuss the affairs of the States was sought to be remedied by limiting the rights of the States to discuss and vote upon such questions as did not relate to internal affairs of British India, but the Princes and their representatives have always been against such distinction being drawn and they insisted that on any matter on which the fate of the Ministry depended they must have the right to decide upon the future of that Government. The constitution has given effect to the point of view of the Princes and set aside the point of view of British India.

This comparison shows that the States are placed by law in a position to control the affairs of British India and by the same law British India is disabled from exercising any influence over the states. That this is the true state of facts must be admitted by all. In other words the Federal Scheme does not help, indeed hinders British India from setting up in motion processes which would result in the democratization of the Indian States. On the other hand it helps the Indian States to destroy democracy in British India.

(3) Federation and Responsibility.

Let us examine the plea of Responsibility. From the stand point of British India it is of more decisive importance than the two other pleas and must be scrutinized more carefully.

It cannot be denied that the Federation has some degree of responsibility. The question is what is the degree of that responsibility and whether within its sphere it is a responsibility which can be called real.

Let us ask, how much responsibility is there in this Federation? To be able to answer this question, you should read Sections 9 and 11 together. By reading them together you will get an idea of the extent of this responsibility. According to these two sections the field of Governmental Authority is divided into two categories. In one category are put four subjects (1) Defence (2)

Ecclesiastical affairs (3) External affairs, and (4) the Administration of Tribal Areas. The rest of the subjects within the executive authority of the Federation are put in another and a separate category. The executive authority for both these categories is vested in the Governor-General. But a distinction is made between them in the matter of Governmental Authority. The Governmental Authority in respect of the four subjects falling in the first category is under the Act the Governor-General in his discretion. The Governmental Authority in respect of the rest of the subjects put in the second category is under the Act, the Governor-General acting on the advice of the Minister. In the case of the first four subjects the Government is not responsible to the Legislature, because the Governor-General in whom the Governmental Authority in respect of these four subjects is vested is not removable by the legislature. In the case of the rest of the subjects the Government is responsible to the Legislature, because the ministers on whose advice the Governmental Authority is exercisable are removable by the Legislature. The responsibility in the Federal scheme is therefore a case of limited responsibility. The responsibility does not extend to Defence and Foreign Affairs which after all are the most important subjects from social, political and financial point of view. The scheme has a close resemblance to dyarchy with the division of subjects into Reserved and

Transferred such as was the basis of the Montagu-Chelmsford Reforms, which was embodied in the Provincial Constitution under the Government of India Act of 1919. The scheme of responsibility in the Federal Constitution under the Act of 1935 is an exact replica of the scheme of responsibility in the Provincial Constitution under the Act of 1919.

Is this responsibility real ? My answer is in the negative. I will give you my reasons. Firstly the field of responsibility besides being limited is not a free field of activity for ministers. To realize how fettered this limited field of responsibility is, we must note certain restraints which have been imposed upon the powers of the Ministers when acting in the the field of responsibility.

The first set of restraints imposed upon the authority of the Ministers when acting in the field of responsibility arises from what are called the special responsibilities of the Governor-General.

There exist another set of restraints on the authority of the Ministers while exercising the Governmental Authority in respect of transferred subjects. To understand this you must understand one special feature of this Federal constitution. The constitution classifies subjects from the stand-point of Governmental Authority and that this classification has resulted in that division of subjects which for brevity's sake may be designated as Transferred and Reserved. The Constitution does not stop here. It goes further and proceeds to divide the category of Transferred subjects into two classes. (1) subjects over which the Ministers' Governmental Authority carries with it administrative control and (2) subjects over which the Governmental Authority of Ministers does not carry with it administrative control. As an illustration of this classification may be mentioned the case of Railways. Railways are a transferred subject. The Governmental Authority of the Ministers extends to Railways. But the Ministers have no right to exercise any administrative control over the Railways. The administrative control over Railways is vested in what is called the Railway Authority. The distinction between Governmental Authority with Administrative Control and Governmental Authority without administrative control is not a distinction without difference. On the other hand the difference between the two positions is very real. That difference is made clear in sub-clause (2) of Section 181 in the matter of Railways. That distinction is the distinction between authority to lay down a policy and competency to act. It is for those who plead for this Federation to say whether there is reality of responsibility in a Scheme of Government where there is a divorce between competence to act and authority to lay down policy.

Two things are clear in regard to this Responsibility in the Federal Scheme. First is that this responsibility is limited in its ambit. Secondly, it is not real because it is fettered by the restraints arising from the special responsibilities of the Governor-General and from the withdrawal from the Ministers Governmental Authority of their competence to act in certain subjects such as the Railways, although they are Transferred subjects.

I have stated that the system of responsibility in the Federal Scheme resembles the system of dyarchy introduced into the Provinces under the Act of 1919. But if the Scheme of responsibility in the Federation was compared with the system of dyarchy introduced into the Provinces it will be found that the former is designed to yield less responsibility than the latter. There are two things introduced in the Federal Scheme which were not to be found in the dyarchy in the Provinces and there existed one thing in the dyarchy which is absent in the Federation. The presence of the two and the absence of one makes this dyarchy in the Federation worse than the dyarchy in the Provinces.

Of the two things that are new in the Federal Scheme one is the principle of special responsibilities of the Governor-General in respect of the Transferred field and the other is the separation between Governmental Authority from administrative control in respect of matters falling within the Transferred field. These two are new things and did not exist in the dyarchical constitution in the provinces.

It may be said that the special responsibilities of the Governor-General is simply another name for the Veto power, that is the power to overrule the Ministers and that even in the English Constitution the King has such a Veto power. On the face of it, this view of special responsibilities of the Governor-General appears to be correct. But in reality it involves a misconception of the conditions and circumstances under which the King's Veto power can be exercised.

To my knowledge no one has explained the relationship of the King and his Ministers in a system of responsible Government better than Macaulay. To use his language :

"In England the King cannot exercise his Veto power unless there is some Minister to take responsibility for the King's act. If there is no Minister to take responsibility the King must yield fight, or abdicate." The Governor-General stands in a different position. He need not yield. He can act even if there is no Minister to take responsibility for his act. That is the difference between the King's Veto and the Veto of the Governor-General. What is however more important to note is that this veto power exists in respect of the Transferred field. In the dyarchical constitution in the Provinces the Transferred field was not subject to such a veto power of the Governor. In other words there were no special responsibilities of the Governor.

If the Governor-General can overrule Ministers even in the Transferred field, question is what substance is there in Ministerial responsibility. I see very little.

The second thing which is new is the separation between Governmental Authority and administrative control. Such a provision did not exist in the dyarchical constitution in the Provinces. In the dyarchical constitution of the Provinces when a subject was transferred both Governmental Authority as well as Administrative control was transferred to the Minister. You will ask yourself what substance is there in Ministerial responsibility if a Minister can only issue directions and cannot control the action taken thereunder? I see very little.

The provision which existed in the dyarachical constitution of the Provinces and which has been omitted from the Federal Constitution relates to the financing of the Reserved subjects. Section 72 D of the old Act of 1919 and Sections 33 and 34 of the present Act may be usefully compared in this connection. Section 72 D sub-section (2) reads as follows:—

"The estimates of annual expenditure and revenue of the Province shall be laid in the form of a statement before the Council in each year, and the proposals of the local Government for the appropriation of provincial revenues and other moneys in any year shall be submitted to the vote of the Council in the form of demands for grants. The Council may assent, or refuse its assent, to a demand, or may reduce the amount therein referred to, either by a reduction of the whole grant or by the omission or reduction of any of the items of expenditure of which the grant is composed." Compare with this Section 34 of the present Act of 1935; sub-section (1) of Section 34 reads as follows:-

"So much of the estimates of expenditure as relates to expenditure charged upon the revenues of the Federation shall not be submitted to the vote of the Legislature, but nothing in this sub-section shall be construed as preventing the discussion in either chamber of the Legislature of any of these estimates other than estimates relating to expenditure referred to in paragraph (a) or paragraph (f) of sub-section (3) of Section 33.

According to Section 33 expenditure charged on the revenues of the Federation includes expenditure on the reserved subjects. On a comparison between the provisions of the two Acts, it is clear that under the old Act no distinctions were made by Section 72 D between Transferred and Reserved subjects, so far as the powers of the Legislature in regard to the granting of were supply concerned and the expenditure on Reserved subjects was not only open to discussion but was also subject to the vote of the Legislature. Under the provisions of Section 34, of the new Act the Federal Legislature can only discuss the expenditure on the reserved subjects but cannot vote upon it. This is a very important distinction. Under the old constitution even the reserved subjects were amenable to the financial powers of the Legislature. Under the present constitution they are independent of the financial powers of the Federal Legislature. It is true that in the Provincial Constitution the vote of the Legislature with regard to expenditure on Reserved subjects was not final. That under a proviso to Section 72 D the Governor ,was given the power "in relation to any such demand to act as if it had been assented to, notwithstanding the withholding of such assent or the reduction of the amount (by the Legislature) if the demand relates to a reserved subject, and the Governor certifies that the expenditure provided for by the demand is essential to the discharge of his responsibility for the subject". It is also true that in the Government of India Act 1935 the amount of expenditure on reserved subjects is fixed to 42 crores. But the same difference exists, namely that under the old constitution the reserved subjects were amenable to the financial control of the Legislature while in the new constitution they are not. This difference is not a small difference. The power to grant supplies is the most effective mode of enforcing the responsibility of the executive. The power of certification might have deprived the Legislature of control over the reserved subjects. But it did not altogether destroy its influence. Under the present constitution the Legislature has not only no control over the reserved subjects but also it cannot have any influence over them. There can therefore be no doubt that there was more responsibility in the dyarchy in the old Provincial Constitution than there is in this dyarchy in the Federation.

The fact that the Executive is not responsible to the Legislature is simply another way of stating that in the Federal Scheme the Executive is supreme. This supremacy of the Executive may be maintained in various ways. It may be maintained by curtailing the powers of the Legislature or it may be maintained by planning the Composition of the Legislature in such a way that the Legislature will always be at the beck and call of the Executive.

The Federal Scheme adopts both these means. In the first place, it limits the powers of the Federal Legislature. I have already described how greatly the Federal Scheme curtails the financial powers of the Federal Legislature. The Federal Legislature has no right to refuse supplies to any expenditure which is declared to be a charge on the revenues.

The Federal Scheme also curtails the Legislative powers of the Federal Legislature. These restraints are specified in section 108 which reads as follows:

"108. (1) Unless the Governor-General in his discretion thinks fit to give his previous sanction, there shall not be introduced into, or moved in, either Chamber of the Federal Legislature, any Bill or amendment which

(a) repeals, amends or is repugnant to any provisions of any Act of Parliament extending to British India; or

(b) repeals, amends or is repugnant to any Governor-General's or Governor's Act, or any ordinance promulgated in his discretion by the Governor-General or a Governor; or

(c) affects matters as respects which the Governor-General is, by or under this Act, required to act in his discretion; or

(d) repeals, amends or affects any Act relating to any police force; or

(e) affects the procedure for criminal proceedings in which European British subjects are concerned; or

(f) subjects persons not resident in British India to greater taxation than persons resident in British India or subjects companies not wholly controlled and managed in British India to greater taxation than companies wholly controlled and managed therein; or

(g) affects the grant of relief from any Federal tax on income in respect of income taxed or taxable in the United Kingdom.

(2) Unless the Governor-General in his discretion thinks fit to give his previous sanction, there shall not be introduced into, or moved in a Chamber of a Provincial Legislature any Bill or amendment which–

(a) repeals, amends, or is repugnant to any provisions of any Act of Parliament extending to British India; or

(b) repeals, amends or is repugnant to any Governor-General's Act, or any ordinance promulgated in his discretion by the Governor-General or

(c) affects matters as respects which the Governor-General is by or under this Act, required to act in his discretion; or

(d) affects the procedure for criminal proceedings in which European British subjects are concerned;

and unless the Governor of Province in his discretion thinks fit to give his previous sanction, there shall not be introduced or moved any Bill or amendment which–

(i) repeals, amends or is repugnant to any Governor's Act, or any ordinance promulgated in his discretion by the Governor; or

(ii) repeals, amends, or affects any Act relating to any police force.

(3) Nothing in this section affects the operation of any other provision in this Act which requires the previous sanction of the Governor-General or of a Governor to the introduction of any Bill or the moving of any amendment."

The Federal Scheme does not stop with merely curtailing the powers of the Federal Legislature as a means of maintaining the supremacy of the Executive. Under it the composition of the Federal Legislature is so arranged that the the Legislature will always be at the beck and call of the Executive. In this connection it is necessary to bear in mind what the actual composition of the Federal Legislature is. As has already been pointed out there are 375 members in the Legislative Assembly and of them 125 have been assigned to the Indian States and 250 to British India. In the Council of State the total is 260 and of them 104 are assigned to the States and 156 are allotted to British India. The seats assigned to the States are to be filled by the Princes by nomination. The seats assigned to British India are to be filled by election. The Federal Legislature is therefore an heterogeneous legislature partly elected and partly nominated.

The first question to be considered is how the Princes' nominees in the Federal Legislature will behave. Will they be independent of the Federal Executive or will they be subservient to it? It is difficult to prophesy. But certain influences which are likely to play a part in the making of these nominations may be noted. It is an indisputable fact that the British Government claims what are called rights of paramountcy over the States. "Paramountcy" is an omnibus term to denote the rights which the Crown can exercise through the Political Department of the Government of India over the States. Among these rights is the right claimed by the Political Department to advise the Indian Princes in the matter of making certain appointments. It is well known that what is called "advice" is a diplomatic term for dictation. There is no doubt that the Political Department will claim the right to advise the Princes in the matter of filling up these places. Should this happen, what would be the result ? The result would be this, that the Princes' representatives would be simply another name for an official block owing allegiance, not to the people and not even to the Princes, but to the Political Department of the Government of India. Two things must be further noted. First is that Paramountcy is outside the Federal Government. That means that the Ministers will have no right to give any advice in the matter of the nomination of the Princes' Representatives and the Legislature will have no right to criticise it. They will be under the control of the Viceroy as distinct from the Governor-General. Secondly, this official block of the Princes is not a small block. In the Lower House a party which has 187 seats can command a majority. In the Upper Chamber a party which has 130 seats can command a majority. In the Lower House the Princes have 125 seats. All that they need is a group of 62 to make a majority. In the Upper Chamber they have 104 ; all that they need is 26. All this vast strength the Executive can command. How can such a Legislature be independent ? The Reserved half can control the Transferred half with this strength in its possession.

How will the representatives of British India behave ? I cannot make any positive statement. But I like it to be borne in mind that in some States there is no such thing as a regular budget and there is no such thing as independent audit and accounts. It would not be difficult for the Princes to purchase support from British India representatives. Politics is a dirty game and British India politicians cannot all be presumed to be beyond corruption and when purchases can be made without discovery the danger is very real.

Look at the Federal Scheme any way you like and analyze it as you may its provisions relating to responsibility, you will see that of real responsibility there is none.

VII. THE BANE OF THE FEDERAL SCHEME.

There is no one who does not recognize that this Scheme for an All Indian Federation is full of defects. A difference of opinion arises only when the question is asked what shall we do about it. The answers given to this question by prominent Indians from time to time disclose that broadly speaking, there are two quite different attitudes to this Federation. There is the attitude of those who think that bad as it is, we should accept the Federation and work it so as to derive whatever good it can yield. On the other hand, there is the attitude of those who think that certain changes must be made in the Constitution of the Federation before it can be accepted and worked. It is agreeable to find that both the Congress as well as the Liberal Federation are one on this issue. Both have declared that certain changes must be made before they will accept to work the Federation.

That this Federation is not acceptable to a large majority of the Indian people is beyond question. The question is in what respects should we require the Constitution to be amended? What are the changes which we should demand? We may take as our starting point the resolutions passed by the Congress and the Liberal Federation relating to this question. The Congress at its session held at Haripura in 1938 passed the following resolution:—

"The Congress has rejected the new Constitution and declared that a constitution for India, which can be accepted by the people, must be based on independence and can only be framed by the people themselves by means of a Constituent Assembly, without interference by any foreign authority. Adhering to this policy of rejection, the Congress has, however, permitted the formation in provinces of Congress Ministries with a view to strengthen the nation in its struggle for independence. In regard to the proposed Federation, no such considerations apply even provisionally or for a period, and the imposition of this Federation will do grave injury to India and tighten the bonds which hold her in subjection to imperialist domination. This scheme of Federation excludes from the sphere of responsibility vital functions of government.

"The Congress is not opposed to the idea of Federation; but a real Federation must, even apart from the question of responsibility consist of free units enjoying more or less the same measure of freedom and civil liberty, and representation by the democratic process of election. The Indian States participating in the Federation should approximate to the provinces in the establishment of representative institutions and responsible government, civil liberties and method of election to the Federal Houses. Otherwise the Federation as it is now contemplated, will, instead of building up Indian unity, encourage separatist tendencies and involve the States in internal and external conflicts.

"The Congress therefore reiterates its condemnation of the proposed Federal Scheme and calls upon the Provincial and Local Congress Committees and the people generally, as well as the Provincial Governments and Ministries, to prevent its inauguration. In the event of an attempt being made to impose it, despite the declared will of the people, such an attempt must be combated in every way and the Provincial Governments and Ministries must refuse to co-operate with it. In case such a contigency arises, the All India Congress Committee is authorised and directed to determine the line of action to be pursued in this regard."

The resolution passed by the National Liberal Federation at its last session held in Bombay was in the following terms:—

> "The National Liberal Federation reiterates its opinion that the Constitution,

especially as regards the Centre as embodied in the Government of India Act 1935, is utterly unsatisfactory and in several respects retrogade. While the National Liberal Federation accepts a federal form of Government for India as the only natural ideal for our country, the Federation considers that vital changes are required in the form of the Federation as laid down in the Act especially in the direction of (a) clearing up the position of the Princes and securing the subjects of States the right of election of states' representatives, (b) doing away with the safeguards regarding the monetary policy and commercial discrimination, (c) introducing direct elections for the members of the Federal Assembly by the Provinces and (d) making Constitution sufficiently elastic so as to enable India to attain Dominion Status within a reasonable period of time.

"The National Liberal Federation considers that the present position when there is an irresponsible government in the Centre coupled with responsible governments in the Provinces is altogether untenable and earnestly urges on Parliament to make immediate changes in the

Federal part of the Constitution so as to make it generally acceptable.

"The Federation is further of opinion that these modifications are essential for the successful working of the Federal Constitution."

Should these changes demanded by the Congress or by the Liberal Federation suffice to alter the present attitude of rejection into one of acceptance of Federation ? Speaking for myself I have no hesitation in saying that the changes asked for in these Resolutions even if they are made will not convert me. To my mind whether the British Parliament is prepared to alter this, that or the other detail of the Federal Scheme immediately is a very unimportant consideration. In the view I take of the matter the objections to the Federal Scheme will not be removed in the least even if the British Parliament will be ready to grant every one of the demands contained in these Resolutions. To me the fundamental question is whether this Federal Scheme is capable of so evolving that in the end India will reach her goal and it is from this point of view that I want you and every one interested to examine the Federal Scheme.

What is the goal of India's political evolution? There does not seem to be any fixity or definiteness about it. The Congress which claims to voice the political aspirations of the Indian people began with good government as its goal. It moved from good government to Self-Government or Responsible Government ; from Responsible Government to Dominion Status and from Dominion Status it advanced to Independence. There the Congress stopped for some time in a mood of self-examination. Then there was a period of vaccilation. Now it seems to have come back to Dominion Status and we shall not be very wrong if we take that to be the goal of India according to the Congress. Now the question is, can the Federal Scheme blossom in due course into Dominion Status ?

Many Indians seem to think that the question of Dominion Status is a matter of gift which lies in the hands of the British Parliament. If the British Parliament were to make up its mind to grant it, nothing can stand in the way. They contend that if India has no hope of Dominion Status, it is because the British Parliament refused to grant it. In support of their opinion they refer to the refusal of The British Parliament to add a Preamble to the Act of 1935 declaring Dominion Status as the goal for India.

It must be granted that the demand for such a preamble was a very proper one. In 1929 Lord Irwin with the consent of all the political parties in the British Parliament declared that the goal of India's political evolution was Dominion Status. What the Indians therefore wanted was not new. It had already been so stated authoritatively by the Governor-General and Viceroy, but the British Government refused to put such a preamble. The refusal was therefore a strange piece of conduct on the part of the British Government. But the grounds urged in support of the refusal were stranger still. The British Government sought to justify their conduct in not having a preamble in those terms on various grounds.

The first ground was that a preamble was a futility and that it had no operative force, but that argument was easily met. All Acts of Parliament have had Preambles expressing the purpose and the intention of Parliament. It is true that it has no legal effect, but all the same Courts have not held that a preamble is a futile thing. On the other hand, wherever there is any doubt with regard to the wording of a section, Courts have always resorted to the preamble as a key to understand the purpose of the enactment and made use of it for resolving any doubtful construction. Driven from this position, the British Government took another position and that was to repeal the Act of 1919 but to retain the Preamble to that Act. This again is a very queer thing. In the first place if the Preamble is a futility, there is no necessity to save the Preamble enacted as part of the Act of 1919. Secondly if the Preamble to the Act of 1919 was a necessity, it should have been enacted afresh as a part of this Act of 1935, which the British Government would not do. Instead it preferred to present the strange spectacle of the head separated from the trunk. The head is now to be found in the repealed Act of 1919 and the trunk is to be found in the present enactment of 1935. In the third place, what the Indian people wanted was a preamble promising Dominion Status and that is what the declaration of Lord Irwin contained. The preamble to the Act of 1919 speaks only of Responsible Government. It does not speak of Dominion Status and the retention of the Preamble to the Act of 1919 was to say the least the silliest business possible.

Why did the British Parliament refuse to enact a Preamble defining Dominion Status as the goal? Why did the British Parliament run from pillar to post rather than grant the demand? The explanation offered is of course the usual one namely, the perfidy of the Albion! My own view is different. The British Parliament did not promise Dominion Status by enacting a Preamble because it realized that it would be beyond its power to fulfil such a promise. What the British Parliament lacked was not honesty. Indeed it was its honesty which led it to refuse to enact such a preamble because it knew that it could not give effect to such a preamble. What it lacked was courage to tell the Indians that the Federal Scheme left no way for Dominion Status.

Why is Dominion Status impossible under the Federal Scheme? It is impossible because it is not possible to have Responsible Government. It must be borne in mind that to reach Dominion Status, India must first attain Responsible Government. To attain Responsible Government the subjects which are reserved must become transferred. That is the first stage in the process of evolution towards Dominion Status.

Some of you will want to know the reasons why I say that the reserved subjects cannot become transferred. They are sure to recall that there were Reserved subjects in the Provincial Scheme as they are in the Federal Scheme and will ask that if the reserved subjects have become transferred in the course of say 20 years what difficulty can there be in the similar things happening in the Federation. As the question is important, I proceed to give my reason. In the first place, the analogy of the Provinces is false. It is important to note why the analogy is false. It is false because in the Provincial Scheme the distinction between the reserved and the transferred subjects was based upon the requirements of administrative efficiency. That the distinction between the reserved and the transferred subjects in the Federal Scheme is based upon legal necessity and not upon administrative efficiency needs no proof. One of the reasons why the Simon Commission did not recommend dyarchy at the Centre was that it felt that administratively it was not possible to divide subjects into two water-tight compartments, one reserved and the other transferred, without affecting the efficiency of all; and the Government of India's despatch on the Simon Commission entirely agreed with that view. The division, therefore, is not administrative in its basis. It is the result of a legal necessity. This is a fundamental distinction and ought never to be lost sight of.

How does this legal necessity arise? I say the legal necessity for treating certain subjects as reserved arises because of the Indian States. I go further and say that there would be no necessity for treating certain subjects as reserved if the Federation was confined to the British India Provinces only. The reservation of certain subjects is a direct consequence of the entry of the Indian States into the Federation.

What is it, in the position of the Indian States which compels certain subjects to be treated as reserved? To be able to answer this question I must first draw your attention to Section 180 of the Government of India Act. Section 180 says :—

> "Any contract made before the commencement of Part III of this Act by or on behalf of the Secretary of State in Council solely in connection with the exercise of the functions of the Crown in its relations with Indian States, shall, as from the commencement of Part III of this Act, have effect as if it had been

made on behalf of His Majesty and references in any such contract to the Secretary of State in Council shall be construed accordingly".

This section gives statutory form to the contention put forward by the Princes before the Butler Committee and accepted by them, that the treaties of the Indian States were with the Crown of England as such and not with the Government of India.

The next step is to note what follows from this theory. Now what follows from this theory is very crucial, but has been unfortunately allowed to pass without due care and attention. The Princes have contended that as treaty relations of the Indian States are with the Crown of England, the duty and responsibility of fulfilling the obligations arising under those treaties lay solely upon the Crown of England and the Crown of England must at all times maintain itself in a position to fulfil those obligations.

What is the obligation which the treaties with the Princes impose upon the Crown of England? The principle of obligation imposed upon the Crown of England and which the Crown of England has undertaken by the treaties is to protect the Princes from internal commotion and external aggression.

How can the Crown fulfil this obligation? The only way, it is argued, that the Crown can fulfill this obligation is to reserve external affairs and the Army under its exclusive control.

You can now understand why I say that the necessity of reserved subjects is due to a legal necessity. That legal necessity flows from the treaty obligations of the Crown and so long as the basis of the treaty relations remains what Section 180 says it is, the reserved subjects cannot become transferred subjects. And as the reserved subjects cannot become transferred, there is no scope even for Responsible Government much less for Dominion Status.

From the analysis I have made of the Constitution, from the stand point of the ultimate goal, few, I believe, will have any hesitation to say that this Constitution is a fixed and rigid constitution. It cannot change and therefore it cannot progress. It is a constitution which is striken at the very base and it is for the people of India to consider whether they will accept it.

I have examined the Constitution from the standpoint of our goal at so considerable a length that I feel I owe you an apology for tiring you. But the attitude of some people towards this question must be my excuse for entering into this subject at such great length. I realize that no Constitution is a perfect constitution. Imperfections there are bound to be. But I think a distinction must be drawn between imperfections and inherent and congenital deficiencies. Imperfections can be removed. But congenital deficiencies cannot be supplied. The demands made in the resolutions of the Congress or of the Liberal Federation, even if granted, will remove the imperfections. But will they remove the deficiencies? I would not mind the imperfections if I was assured that there are no deficiencies. The greatest deficiency in the Constitution is that it will not lead to Dominion Status. Neither the Congress nor the Liberal Federation seems to be aware that this deficiency exists. Their demands have no relation to the goal of India's political evolution. They do not even mention it. It is surprising that Congressmen should have become so enamoured of the prospect of seizing political power that their demands against the British Government should not even contain a declaration from the British Government in this behalf. But if Congressmen forget, the people of India cannot and should not. To do so would be fatal. It would be fatal as much for an individual as for a people to forget that a stage on the way is not the home and to follow the way without knowing whether it leads homewards or not is to misdirect one-self and fall into a ditch.

You must not misunderstand me. I am not an impatient idealist. I am not condemning the gradualist, who is prepared to wait and take thing by instalments, although the gradualist, who has a valid claim for a rupee, demands an anna and proclaims a great victory when he gets a pie, must become an object of pity. All I want is that if circumstances force us to be gradualists we must not fail to be realists. Before accepting an instalment we should examine it carefully and satisfy ourselves that it contains an acknowledgment of the whole claim. Otherwise, as often happens what is good for the moment turns out to be the enemy of the better.

Some of you will ask, how can India secure Dominion Status. My answer is India will get Dominion Status only if the Princes, who join the Federation, consent to its being granted. If the Princes object to the grant of Dominion Status to India, then India cannot get Dominion Status. The Federation places the strings of India's political evolution in the hands of the Princes. The destiny of India will be controlled by the Princes.

This view of the future will strike as very strange to a great many of you. We are all saturated with Dicey's dictum regarding the Sovereignty of Parliament. We all have learned from him that Parliament is supreme, that it is so supreme that it can do anything except make man a woman and woman a man. It would not be unnatural if some of you ask how can the Princes stand in the way when the British Parliament is supreme. It will take some effort on your part to accept the proposition that the British Parliament has no supremacy over the Indian Federation. Its authority to change the Federal Constitution now embodied in the Government of India Act is strictly limited.

Indian politicians have expressed their sense of sorrow and resentment over the fact that the Indian Legislatures have not been given by the Act any constituent powers.

Under the Government of India Act neither the Federal Legislature, nor the Provincial Legislatures have any powers of altering or amending the constitution. The only thing, which the Act by virtue of Section 308 does, is to permit the Federal Legislature and the Provincial Legislatures to pass a resolution recommending any change in the constitution, and make it obligatory upon the Secretary of State to place it before both Houses of Parliament. This is contrary to the provisions contained in the Constitutions of the United States, Australia, the German Federation and Switzerland. There is no reason why constituent power should not have been given within certain defined limits to the Legislatures in India when they were fully representative of all sections and of all interests. Be that as it may, the fact remains that the Indian Legislatures cannot make any changes in constitution, not even in the franchise, much less in making the reserved subjects transferred. The only authority which can change the Constitution is of course the British Parliament. But very few seem to be aware of the fact that even Parliament has no powers to alter the Federal Constitution. This, however, is the truth and the sooner we all realize it the better.

From this point of view the importance of Schedule II cannot be overestimated. I am sorry, it has not received the attention which it deserves. Schedule II is not only a charter but is also a chart along which the Constitution can move. The whole Schedule is worth careful study. What does Schedule II say? Schedule II says that certain provisions of the Government of India Act may be amended by Parliament and that certain other provisions of the Act shall not be amended by Parliament. That is simply another way of saying that Parliament is not supreme and that its right to alter the Constitution is limited.

What would happen if Parliament did amend those provisions of the Act which Schedule II says shall not be amended by Parliament? The answer, which Schedule II gives, is that such an Act will have the effect of 'affecting' the accession of the States to the Federation, which means it will have the effect of destroying the binding character of the Instrument of Accession. In other words, if Parliament amended any of the provisions of the Act, which Schedule II says shall not be amended, the Princes would get the right to secede from the Federation. I am aware that some eminent lawyers have taken a different view. They hold that the Princes, once they come into the Federation, cannot go out of it. I have mentioned my view for what it is worth and I will say that my view is not altogether baseless.

At any rate the Solicitor-General and Secretary of State gave the same interpretation, as I am giving, in the House of Commons, when the Government of India Bill was being discussed.

The Solicitor-General said :—

> "The States will only agree to federate in a structure which within limits, is definite and certain and obviously we could not completely alter the structure afterwards. The purpose of this clause is to lay down those matters which can be altered without being regarded as fundamental or as impinging on the Instrument of Accession." ...... "If the structure were to be altered in fundamental respects, of course the States would clearly have the right to say "This is not the Federation to which we have acceded."

The Secretary of State said :—

> "If you amend the parts of the Bill which affect the States, obviously you would be altering the conditions on which they

have acceded and that would certainly create a situation in which the Princes could rightly claim that their Instrument of Accession had been altered. It certainly means that we cannot amend any part of the Bill which affects what is virtually the treaties under which the Princes come in. If we make a change in the Bill as to strike at the basis of their Instrument of Accession then obviously, the agreement has been broken between the Princes and Parliament and the Princes are free".

"It will be accepted by every one that under the general scheme of the Bill the States, when they are asked to federate are entitled to know with certainty certain aspects at any rate, of the Federation to which they are to accede. It would be an absurd position if having said to a State this month, "Will you accede to a Federation," it was possible next month for this House to alter in some fundamental respects the provisions of the Federation to which the State was held to have acceded. Therefore, some schedule of this kind is necessary. It is a sorting out of the various parts of the Bill which should be capable of amendment without in any sense altering from the point of view of the States the constitutional machinery to which they have acceded. The scheme of the schedule is to set out the provisions of the Act, the amendment whereof is not to affect the validity of the Instrument of Accession of a State.

"One sees set out those parts of the Bill the amendment of which is not to affect the validity of the Instrument of Accession of a State, and on the opposite side there are set out those subjects the amendment of which, would affect the validity of accession. In drawing up a schedule of this kind one has to proceed the with great care in defining what are the legitimate matters on which the Rulers of a State are entitled to ask that there shall be no amendment without their consent. Of course there will be borderline cases. There could be minor amendments, which would not really make any great difference to the existing position, and it would be very unreasonable if the States took objection to such amendments and said, "We are going to stand on our rights on this point as affecting the validity of our Instrument of Accession." It is right that any matter which really affects what I may call the general balance of powers, the questions of the reservation of subjects of executive control and of matters which can be dealt with by the Governor-General in his discretion, matters which are vital to the architecture of the Federation to which the States are asked to accede, should not be amended without their assent.

"The whole area of the special powers vested in the Governor-General is one of the essential features of the Federation. That is one part where the States are entitled to say "That is a change" or "That is altered." But this does not in any way check for all time the development of India. These are to be the subject--matter of negotiations with the States, because, in effect, they will produce a Federation of a different kind from that to which the State has acceded."

Therefore to the question what would happen if Parliament did make such changes which by virtue of Schedule II are treated as changes which will affect the Instrument of Accession the answer is that the Princes will get a right to walk out of the Federation. In other words, the consequence of any such change would be to break up the Federation.

What are the changes which cannot be made without affecting the Instrument of Accession ? I will draw your attention to some of the provisions which Schedule II says cannot be amended by Parliament without affecting the Instrument of Accession. According to Schedule II no changes in the Constitution can be made which relate to (1) the exercise by the Governor-General of the executive authority of the Federation; (2) the definition of the functions of the Governor-General; (3) the executive authority of the Federation; (4) the functions of the Council of Ministers and the choosing and summoning of ministers and their tenure of office; (5) the power of the Governor-General to decide whether he is entitled to act in his discretion or exercise his individual judgment; (6) the functions of the Governor-General with respect to external affairs and defence; (7) the special responsibilities of the Governor-General relating to the peace and tranquility of India or any part thereof; (8) the financial stability and credit of the Federal Government; (9) the rights of the Indian States and the rights and dignity of their Rulers: (10) the discharge of his functions by or under the Act in his discretion or in the exercise of his individual judgment; (11) His Majesty's Instrument of Instructions to the Governor-General; and (12) the superintendence of the Secretary of State in the making of the rules for the Governor-General in his discretion for the transaction of and the securing of transmission to him of information with respect to, the business of the Federal Government.

Schedule II is a very extensive collection of constitutional don'ts. I have given just a few of them. They will however be sufficient to show how limited is the authority of Parliament to make changes in the Constitution.

Why is the authority of Parliament limited? To understand this it is necessary to note the exact limits of the authority of Parliament. According to law the authority of Parliament to legislate extends only to countries which are the Dominions of the King. The States did not form part of the Dominions of the King and none of them not even the finest of them was subject to the legislative authority of Parliament. The Government of India Act makes no change in this status of the States. The States remain foreign territories inspite of the Federation, and as they were before Federation. This is the most extra-ordinary state about the Indian Federation, namely that the different units are as between themselves foreign states. As the Act does not make the States Dominions of the King, Parliament gets no right to legislate about them. Parliament derives its authority over the States from the Instrument of Accession. That being so, the authority of Parliament cannot but be limited to what is transferred to it by the States through their instruments. To use the language of the Privy Council itself, as the stream can rise no higher than its source, similarly, Parliament cannot have powers over the States greater than those given to them by the Instrument of Accession. This explains why the authority of Parliament to amend the Constitution is limited.

The analysis made so far shows that the authority of Parliament to change is limited by the Instrument of Accession and that for any excess of authority, there must be prior consent given by the Princes. As a legal effect of the provisions of the Act it may not be shocking. But consider the fact that the provisions in regard to which Parliament has no power to change include those that relate to the transposition of such subjects as Defence and External affairs from the category of Reserved to that of the Transferred and that it will not have that power unless the Princes consent expressly to confer that authority on Parliament and permit it to do so. You will be in a position to realize how grave are going to be the consequences of this Federation. The establishment of the Federation means that the mastery has gone from the hands of Parliament into the hands of Princes. This Federation makes the Princes the arbiters of our destiny. Without their consent India cannot politically advance.

Other consequences of this Federation might also be noted. I will just refer to one. It is that this Federation, if accepted will weaken the position of British Indians in their struggle for change. Hitherto, in the struggle between the

Indian people and the British Parliament the latter was always the weaker party. It had nothing to oppose the right of the people to change except its will. After the Federation the position is bound to be reversed. The Indian people would be in a weaker position and Parliament would be in a stronger position. After the Federation, Parliament would be in a position to say that it is willing to grant the demand for change but that its authority to change is limited and that before making any demand for change, Indians should obtain the consent of the Princes. There is nothing to prevent Parliament from taking this stand.

What reply would Indians be able to give if they once accept the Federation and thereby admit the implications underlying it ?

VIII. THE FATALITY OF FEDERATION.

What shall we do with the Indian States? That is a question that is often asked. Some people with Republican faith in them desire their total abolition. Those who do not care for forms of Government will reject this view. But even they must abide by the consideration that what works best is best. Can the Indian States be said to work best? I do not know that there is any body, who will be prepared to give an affirmative answer, at any rate an affirmative answer which will apply to all States. The internal administration of the States is a bye-word for mismanagement and maladministration. Very few States will escape this charge.

The people are always asking as to why there should be this mismanagement and maladministration in the States. The usual answer is that it is the consequence of Personal Rule. Everywhere the demand made is that Personal Rule should be replaced by Popular Government. I have grave doubts about the efficacy of this demand. I do not think that in a large majority of cases the substitution of Popular Government will be any cure for the ills of the State subjects. For, I am sure that the evils arise as much from the misrule of the Ruler as they arise from want of resources. Few have any idea as to how scanty are the resources of the Indian States.

Let me give you a few facts. Out of the total of 627 States there are only ten with an annual revenue above 1 crore. Of these ten, five have just about a crore, three have between 2 and $2\frac{1}{4}$ crores. One has just about $3\frac{1}{4}$ crores and only one has a revenue just about 8 crores. There are nine with a revenue ranging between 1 crore and 50 lakhs. About twelve have a revenue ranging between 50 to 25 lakhs. Thirty have a revenue varying between 25 lakhs and 10 lakhs. The rest of the 566 have an annual revenue which is less than 10 lakhs. This does not, however, give an idea of how small are some of the States which fall below 10 lakhs. A few illustrations may therefore be given. Among these 566 States there is one with a revenue of Rs. 500/- and a population of 206 souls. Another with a revenue of Rs. 165 and a population of 125; another with a revenue of Rs. 136 and a population of 239, another with a revenue of 128 and a population of 147 and another with a revenue of Rs. 80 and a population of 27. Each one of these is an Autonomous State, even the one with a revenue of Rs. 80 and a population of 27 !

The Autonomy of these States means that each one must take upon itself the responsibility to supply to its subjects all the services which relate to matters falling under law and order such as revenue, executive and judicial and all the services which affect public welfare such as education, sanitation, roads etc. We in Bombay with our 12 crores of revenue are finding it difficult to maintain a civilized standard of administration. Other Provinces with equally large revenue are finding the same difficulty. How then can these small tiny states with a revenue of few hundreds and a population of few thousands cater to any of the wants which a civilized man must have his Government satisfy in full measure? With the best of motives and given an ideal prince the task is hopeless.

The only way out is to reorganize the whole area occupied by the Indian States. The proper solution would be to fix an area of a certain size and of certain revenue and to constitute it into a New Province and to pension off the rulers now holding any territory in that area. Only such States should be retained in whose case by measure of area and revenue it can be said that they by reason of their resources are in a position to provide a decent standard of administration. Those which cannot satisfy the test must go. There is no other way. This is not merely what might be done. I say, to do this is our duty and a sacred duty.

I know some will think of the hereditary right of the Prince to rule over his territory. But I ask, what is more important, the right of the Prince or the welfare of the people? I am sure that even the best friends of the States will not say that the rights of the Prince are more important than the welfare of the people. Which should give way, if the two are in conflict? There again, I am sure that even the best friends of the States will not say that the welfare of the people should be sacrificed for the sake of maintaining the rights of the Prince.

The question of the reorganization of the Indian States is not a political question. As I look at it, it is a purely administrative question. It is also an inevitable question. Because, not to tackle it is to condemn the people of the States-and there are millions of them-perpetually to a life of misery and insecurity. The way I suggest is not a revolutionary way. To pension off a Prince and to annex his territory is a legal way and can fall under the principles with which we are familiar under the Land Acquisition Act which allows private rights and properties to be acquired for public purposes.

Unfortunately, the question of the Indian States has not been tackled from this point of view so far. The question that I want to place before you is, and it is a very important question, "Will it be open to you to tackle this question after the

Federation is established ?" I say no. You will perhaps ask why. How does this conclusion follow ?

I have already pointed out that with regard to the entry into the Federation, the Provinces and the States stand on a different footing. The Provinces have no choice. They must agree to be the units of the Federation. The States have a choice. They may join the Federation or they may refuse to join the Federation. That is so from the standpoint of the Provinces and from the standpoint of the States. What is the position from the standpoint of the Federation ? Has the Federation any choice in the matter of the admission of the States ? Can the Federation refuse to admit a State into the Federation ? The answer is no. The Federation has no right to refuse. The State has a right to enter the Federation. But the Federation has no right to refuse admission at any rate for the first 20 years. That is the position. Now what does the admission of a State into the Federation mean ? In my view the admission of a State into the Federation means recognition of the sovereign status of the State. Recognition of its sovereign status means the recognition of its indestructibility which means its right to the integrity of its territory and to guaranteeing of its powers of internal administration. This would apply even to the state with a population of 27 and revenue of Rs. 80. These being the implications of the admission of a State in the Federation, I am perfectly justified in suggesting that the territorial reorganization of the Indian States will not be possible after the establishment of the Federation and the people of the Indian States will be for ever doomed to misrule and mal-administration.

Can British India do anything in the matter now? I think British India is not in a position to do anything in the matter. If British India could have secured Responsible Government for itself, it might have been in a position to dictate which State should be admitted and on what terms. It would have been in a position to make the reorganization of the States territory into tolerably big units as a condition precedent for their entry into the Federation. Unfortunately British India has no Responsible Government. Indeed its right to Responsible Government at the Centre is denied and is made dependent upon the entry of the States. 'No States, no responsibility' has now become the fate of British India. That being the position of British India, British India is not in a position to make terms with the States as she would have been able to do if she had Responsible Government. That is why I have said - and that is why I have always maintained - that British Indians should first ask for a Federation and Responsibility confined to British India. Once that is obtained, the path for an All India

Federation on the basis of freedom and good government all round will become possible. That possibility will be gone if this Federation comes into being.

I have already drawn your attention to some of the deformities of the Federal Scheme. What I have now drawn attention to is more than a deformity. It is a fatality of the Federation. So far as the States people are concerned, it is a decree of fate. It is something which they will never be able to escape once it is executed.

The States problem is one which, I believe could be solved by the Paramount Power along the lines I have suggested or along any other line consistently with the welfare of the people, if it wishes to do so. Paramountcy is like the Trimurti of Hindu Theology. It is Brahma because it has created the States. It is Vishnu because it preserves them. It is Shiva because it can destroy them. Paramountcy has played all these parts in different times in relation to the States. At one time, it played the part of Shiva. It has now been playing the part of Vishnu. To play the part of Vishnu with regard to the States is from the point of view of the good of the people the cruelest act. Should British India be a party to it? It is for you to consider.

IX. FEDERATION WITHOUT THE STATES.

There is another point of view from which the case for Federation is argued. I must now proceed to examine that argument.

It is argued that the constitution creates Autonomous Provinces. The Autonomy of the Provinces means independence and therefore disruption of the Unity of British India. This must be counteracted. Some binding force must be provided so that the Provinces may be held together and unity and uniformity built up for the last hundred of years as a result of British administration is preserved intact in fundamentals if not in details.

The argument is quite sound, if it only means that the creation of Autonomous Provinces makes the creation of a Central Government a necessity. This proposition I am sure will command universal assent. In all the Round Table Conferences the late Sir Mahomad Iqbal was the only delegate who was against the establishment of a Central Government. Every other delegate irrespective of caste or creed differed from him. They asserted that with the creation of Autonomous Provinces the establishment of a Central Government was a categorial imperative and that without it autonomy would result in anarchy.

But the argument goes beyond its legitimate scope. It seeks to justify the establishment of a Central Government for All India. The argument which can justify the establishment of a Central Government for British India is used to justify a Central Government for the whole of India. And the question that you have to consider is whether the creation of Autonomous Provinces in British India can justify a Central Government for the whole of India including the Indian States. My contention is that the creation of Autonomous Provinces does not require the creation of a Central Government for the whole of India.

The establishment of Autonomous Provinces in British India will call for two things: (1) That there shall be a Central Government for British India and that the form of that Central Government must be federal and not unitary. The essence of Federation lies in the division or allocation of Legislative and Executive Powers between the Central Government and the Units by law. The Powers of the Units and the Centre are defined and demarcated and the one is not entitled to invade the domain of the other. Autonomy of the Provinces means that their powers are defined and vested in them. To make Provincial Autonomy real the Powers of the Central Government must also be limited, otherwise it would be in a position to invade the domain of the Provinces. To put it simply, autonomy means definition and delimitation of Powers by law and wherever there is definition and delimitation of powers between two Political Bodies there is and there must be Federation. You will now understand why I said that all that Provincial Autonomy demands is that the Central Government for British India shall be Federal in form. It does not justify all India Federation. Why is it necessary to bring in the States still remains to be answered and those who plead for this All-India Federation as distinct from British India Federation must answer this question.

As I said all that is necessary is that the Central Government for British India shall be Federal in form and this fact has been recognized by the Constitution.

Many seemed to have failed to notice that the Government of India Act 1935 establishes two distinct Federations. One is a federation which is a federation of the Provinces of British India and another which is a Federation of British Indian Provinces and the Indian States. It is surprising that so many should have missed so important a fact. That the Government of India Act establishes two federations is beyond dispute. To those who have any doubt they should read Part III and Part XIII together and Part II and Part III together. Part II and Part III reveal that there is an All-India Federation and lay down the constitution of that Federation. Part III and Part XIII reveal that there is a

Federation of British India Provinces apart from the States and lay down the Constitution of that Federation. That Part XIII relates to provisions which are called transitional does not make the British India Scheme any the less a Federation, because the law is law whether it is for a limited period or for all times.

That the Act establishes a Federation for British India Provinces and also an All-India Federation cannot be denied. What is the difference between these two Federations? Is there any difference in the Legislative Powers of the Federation? The answer is no. The Federal Legislative List remains the same whether the Federation that is in operation is British India Federation or the All-India Federation. The Concurrent list also remains the same whether the Federation in operation is one or the other.

Is there any difference in Financial Powers? The answer again is no.

The Powers of taxation remain the same whether it is an All-India Federation or British India Federation.

Is there any change in the Judicial organization of the Federation? There is none. Federal Court is as much necessary for the All-India Federation as for British India Federation.

How do these two Federations differ? The two differ in one respect only. To find out this difference you should compare Section 313 with Section 8. The comparison will show that if the Federation is a British India Federation the Executive Authority of the Federation will be the Governor - General in Council and if the federation is an All-India Federation the Executive Authority in transferred matters to be the Governor-General acting on the advice of Ministers responsible to the Legislature. In other words while there is British India Federation only there is no responsibility at the Centre so long as there is no All-India Federation.

This means that the entry of the States is a condition precedent for the grant of responsibility to British India. You will therefore ask, why is the entry of the States so essential ?

All Federations have come into existence as a result of some danger from outside affecting the safety and integrity of the Units. The States of North America federated because of the fear of subjugation of the States by British Imperialism. The Provinces of Canada federated because of the danger of invasion or absorption by the United States. The Australian Colonies federated because of the danger of invasion by Japan. It is obvious that the Indian Federation is not the result of any such circumstance. There is no new invader on the border of India waiting to pounce upon both British India and the Indian States. Nor is this Federation necessary for bringing about peace between British India and the Indian States. It matters not that British India is under the sovereignty of the Crown and the Indian States are under the suzerainty of the Crown. So far as foreign relations are concerned, and they include peace and war, the two are subordinate to one and the same authority namely the Crown. That is the reason why the two have been at peace. That is the reason why they will not be and cannot be at war. Prevention of external aggression or the maintenance of internal peace cannot be the motive for this All India Federation. What then can be the motive of this Federation? Why are the States invited to enter into this Federation? Why is their entry made a condition precedent for responsibility at the Centre? To put it bluntly, the motive is to use the Princes to support imperial interests and to curb the rising tide of democracy in British India. I should like to have another explanation, if there is any. I see none. That the Princes are wanted in the Federation to serve the ends of British Imperialism is beyond question. The Secretary of State for India speaking in Parliament during the course of the debate on the Government of India Bill admitted that "we should all welcome the entry into the Central Government of India of a great force of stability and imperial feeling represented by the Princes." While the suppression of democracy in British India may not be the motive I am sure that that will be the consequence of the entry of the Princes into the Federation.

What a price has been paid for the entry of the Federation! I do not wish to repeat what I have said. If you will re-call what I have said regarding the discrimination which has been made in favour of the Princes in the matter of representation, taxation, administration, legislation etc., you will know what benefits have been conferred, what rights have been surrendered and what immunities have been granted by British India to induce the Princes to come into the Federation. And what has British India got in return?

If the Federal Constitution had provided full responsible Government, there would have been some compensation to British India for the price it has paid to the Princes for their joining the Federation. But British India has not got any responsibility worth the name. What British India has got is a system of responsibility halved in part and mutilated in substance by conditions and restraints. Not only British India has not been able to secure responsibility at the Centre commensurate with the sacrifices it has made for making the Federation easy for the Princes, but it has lost its claim for Dominion Status in its own right and independently of the Princes. Many people do not know what British India has lost and stands to lose in this business of an All India Federation.

The new Constitution is the result of the struggle of the people of British India. It is the agitation and the sufferings of the people of British India which was the compelling force behind this constitution. What was the right which the people of British India were claiming for themselves? As I have said, their first claim was good government in British India. Next they claimed self-government, that is responsible government for British India. Lastly, they claimed Dominion Status for British India. Each one of these claims have been accepted by the British Parliament. In 1917 the British Parliament accepted the goal of Responsible Government. In 1929 the English Nation accepted the goal of Dominion Status. Now it must be emphasised that each time the claim was made, it was made in the name of the people of British India. Each time it was accepted in relation to the people of British India. What is going to be the position of British India as a result of the Federation? The position of British India is that they can never get any responsibility at the Centre unless the Princes come into the Scheme. That means that British India has lost its right to claim Responsible Government for itself in its own name and independently of the Princes. This right was a vested right because it was the result of a claim made and accepted. That right has been lost because British India is made dependent for the realization of its destiny upon the wishes of the States. Of the two parts of this Federation, British India is the progressive part and the States form the unprogessive part. That the progressive part should be tied up to the chariot of the unprogressive and its path and destiny should be made dependent upon the unprogressive part constitutes the most tragic side of this Federation.

For this tragedy you have to blame your own national leaders. Fortunately for me I am not one of your national leaders. The utmost rank to which I have risen is that of a leader of the Untouchables. I find even that rank has been denied to me. Thakkar Bappa, the left hand man of Mahatma Gandhi-I call him left hand man only because Vallabbhai Patel is the right hand man-very recently said that I was only the leader of the Mahars. He would not even allow me the leadership of the Untouchables of the Bombay Presidency. Whether what Thakkar Bapa said was said by him out of malice or out of love of truth does not worry me. For politics is not my first love nor is national leadership the goal of my life. On the other hand, when I see what disasters your national leaders have brought upon this country I feel relieved to know that I am not included in that august crowd. Believe me when I say that some of your national leaders were thoroughly unprepared for the job of constitution-making. They went to the Round Table Conference without any comparative study of constitutions and could propound no solutions to problems with which they were presented. Others who were undoubtedly competent to tackle the problem were like little children so charged with the ideal of Federation that they never cared to see whether what they were shaping was a real federation or a fraud in the name of Federation. This tragedy is entirely due to wrong leadership. I do not know if the steps taken can be retraced and whether the lost ground can be regained. But I think it is a right thing that the people of British India should know what they have lost. They have a federation of their own and they have right to demand responsibility for their federation.

There is another reason why it would be desirable to have a Federation of British India only. A Federation of British India and of the Indian States cannot work harmoniously. There are two elements which I am sure will produce a conflict between British India and the Indian States. The first element arises out of the difference in the position of the representatives of British India and those of the Indian States. The representatives of British India will be free men. The representatives of the Indian States will be bondmen of the Political Department. The sources of mandate of these two sets of representatives in the Federal Legislature will be different. The British India representatives will be engaged in extending the authority of the Ministers. The States representatives are sure to act and will be made to act so as to lend support to the authority of the Governor-General as against the Ministers. This conflict is inevitable and it is sure to embitter the feelings of British India towards the Indian States. This was precisely what happened in the last regime in the Provinces. The feelings of the elected members towards the nominated members in the old Provincial Councils were certainly unfriendly. This experience I am sure will be repeated in the Federal Legislature. That it should be so is very natural when one section of the House feels that the other section has been brought in to thwart its wishes and is acting as the tool of some power outside the control of the Legislature. This is one element of disharmony. The other element of disharmony is the disparity in the position of British India and the Indian States under the Federation. Equality before law is a precious thing. But not all people value it for the same reason. Most cherish it as an ideal. Few realize why it is crucial. Equality before the law compels men to make common cause with all others similarly affected. Whereas if there is no equality, if some are favoured and others are burdened, those specially favoured not only refuse to join those who are burdened, in the struggle for equality but actually take sides against them. A Dictator might, as the kings did in the olden times, pull out one by one the teeth of a few without necessarily exciting the resentment of the other people. On the contrary, the others will join in the raid. But suppose a law was made that all must contribute as much money as the dictators ask for under penalty of their teeth being drawn out all would rise in opposition. There is no equality between British India and the Indian States under the Federation. Indian States enjoy many benefits and many exemptions which are denied to British India. This is particularly so in the matter of taxation. There is bound to be great acrimony between the representatives of British India and those of the Indian States as to who should bear the load of taxation first. Patriotism vanishes when you touch a man's pocket and I am sure that the States representatives will prefer their own financial interest to the necessities of a common front to make the executive responsible to the Legislature.

What is the use of housing British India and the Indian States under one edifice if the result is to make them·quarrel with each other ?

There is a complete dissimilarity between the forms of Government prevalent in British India and the Indian States and the principles underlying the two. These dissimilarities need not produce any antagonism between the Indian States and British India if the two continue to evolve in their separate spheres. So long as the form of Government in the Indian States does not become a factor in the decision of affairs which affects British India, British India can tolerate those forms of Government however antiquated they may be.

But the Federation makes them a factor and a powerful factor and British India cannot remain indifferent to them. Indeed the forging of the Federation will compel British India to launch a compaign in sheer self-interest for revolutionising the forms of Government prevalent in the Indian States.

This will be the inevitable result of this Federation. Is this a consummation which the States devoutly wish for ? This is a question they will have to consider.

Does British India welcome this prospect ? Speaking for myself I will not. It would be impossible to wage war on so vast a front. The States are too numerous to allow concentrated attack. The States being a part of the structure, you cannot attack them and justify your attack as a Constitutional Act. Secondly, why put yourself in this difficulty ? Sometimes it turns out that a man thinks that he is buying property when as a matter of fact he is buying litigation. For British India to accept this Federation is like buying trouble. Thirdly, this Constitution is a settlement from which Dominion Status is most rigidly excluded not only for the present but also for the future as well.

Looked at from any point of view, the wisest course seems to me that leaving the States where they are, British India should proceed on its own evolution and Federation for itself.

X. FEDERATION FROM DIFFERENT POINTS OF VIEW.

Different people are looking at this Federation from different points of view. There is the point of view of the Princes. There is the point of view of the Hindus and the Muslims and the Congress. There is also the point of view of the Merchant and the Trader. The point of view of each one of these is of course the result of their particular interests.

What is the interest of the Princes in this Federation? To understand the motives of the Princes you must go back to the Butler Committee. The Princes had been complaining of the encroachment of the Political Department of the Government of India upon their treaty rights under the doctrine of paramountcy. The Princes were insisting that the Political Department had no greater right against the States except those that were given by the treaties subsisting between them and the British Government. The Political Department on the other hand claimed that in addition to the rights referable to the treaties, the Crown had also rights which were referable to political usages and customs. To adjudicate upon this dispute, the Secretary of State agreed to appoint the Butler Committee. The Princes had hoped that the Butler Committee would accept their contentions and limit the scope of paramountcy to the rights referable to the treaties. Unfortunately for the Princes they were disappointed, because the Butler Committee reported that the Paramountcy was paramount and that there could be no definition or delimitation of it. This decision of the Butler Committee meant a complete subordination of the Princes to the Political Department of the Government of India and the Princes were in search of an escape from this unfortunate position in which they were placed and they found, and quite rightly, that the only solution which can enable them to escape the tyranny of the Political Department was the Federation; because to the extent to which the Federal authority prevailed, the authority of the Political Department would vanish and as the Federal authority could only be exercised by a Federal Legislature and a Federal Executive and as they would have sufficient voice in the Federal Legislature and the Federal Executive they thought of federation. The federal solution of their problem offered two advantages to the Princes. The first was that it would secure to the States internal autonomy which they were very anxious to have, for it is of the essence of federating units to retain in their own hands all powers save those which they themselves have willingly delegated to a common centre and over which they themselves possess a share in the control. The second advantage of the Federation was that Paramountcy would disappear to the extent of the Federal authority. The motive of the Princes, therefore, was selfish and their primary aim was to get rid as much as possible of the authority of the Political Department of the Government of India. This was one of the primary interests of the Princes. The Princes had another interest to safeguard. That was to preserve their sovereignty, their powers of civil and military government as much as possible. They wanted to make the Federation as thin as possible so that it might not impinge upon them very hard. The interest of the Princes is twofold. They wanted to escape Paramountcy. Secondly they did not want to subject themselves too much to the authority of the Federation. In looking at the Federation, the Princes keep two questions before them. How far will this Federation enable them to escape the tyranny of Paramountcy? Secondly, how far does this Scheme of Federation take away their sovereignty and their powers of internal government? They want to draw more under the former and give less under the latter.

The Muslims had an interest which not only coloured their whole vision but made it so limited that they did not care to look at anything else. That interest was their interest as a minority. They knew only one means of protecting themselves against the Hindu majority. That was to ask for reservation of seats with separate electorates and weightage in representation. In 1930 they discovered that there was another and a more efficacious method of protecting the Muslim minorities. That was to carve out new Provinces in which Muslims would be in a majority and Hindus in a minority as a counter-blast to Provinces with Hindus as a majority and Muslims as a minority. They hit upon this system because they felt such as a system of balance of Provinces would permit the Muslims in the Muslim majority Provinces to hold the Hindu minorities in their Provinces as hostages for the good behaviour of the Hindu majorities in the Provinces in which the Muslims were in a minority. The creation of Muslim majority Provinces and to make them strong and powerful was their dominant interest. To accomplish this they demanded the separation of Sindh and the grant of responsible government to the North West Frontier Province so that the Muslims could have a command of four Provinces. To make the Provinces strong they insisted on making the Centre weak. As a means to this end the Muslims demanded that residuary powers should be given to the Provinces and the Hindu representation in the Centre should be reduced by giving the Muslims not only 1/3 seats from the total fixed for British India but also 1/3 from the total assigned to the Princes.

The Hindus as represented by the Hindu Mahasabha were concerned with only one thing. How to meet what they called the menace of the Musalmans ? The Hindu Mahasabha felt that the accession of the Princes was an accretion to the Hindu strength. Everything else was to them of no consequence. Its point of view was Federation at any cost.

The next class whose point of view is worthy of consideration is the Indian Commercial community. The commercial community is no doubt a small community in a vast country like India, but there can be no doubt about it that the point of view of this community is really more decisive than the point of view of any other community. This community has been behind the Congress. It is this community which has supplied the Congress the sinews of war and it knows that having paid the piper it can call for the tune. The commercial community is primarily interested in what is called commercial discrimination and the lowering of the exchange Ratio. It was a very narrow and limited point of view. The Indian Commercial Community is out to displace Europeans from Trade and Commerce and take their place. This it claims to do in the name of nationalism. It wants the right to lower the exchange rate and make profit in its foreign trade. This also it claims to do in the name of nationalism. Beyond getting profits to themselves the Merchants and Traders have no other consideration.

What shall I say about the Congress? What was its point of view? I am sure I am not exaggerating or misrepresenting facts when I say that the Congress point of view at the Round Table Conference was that the Congress was the only party in India and that no body else counted and that the British should settle with the Congress only. This was the burden of Mr. Gandhi's song at the Round Table Conference. He was so busy in establishing his own claim to recognition by the British as the dictator of India that he forgot altogether that the important question was not, with whom the settlement should be made but what were to be the terms of that settlement. As to the terms of the settlement, Mr. Gandhi was quite unequal to the task. When he went to London he had forgotten that he would have before him not those who go to him to obtain his advice and return with his blessings but persons who would treat him as a lawyer treats a witness in the box. Mr. Gandhi also forgot that he was going to a political conference. He went there as though he was going to a Vaishnava Shrine singing the Narsi Mehta's Songs. When I think of the whole affair I am wondering if any nation had ever sent a representative to negotiate the terms of a national settlement who was more unfitted than Mr. Gandhi.

How unfit Mr. Gandhi was to negotiate a settlement becomes evident when one realizes that this Ambassador of India was ready to return to India with only Provincial Autonomy when as a matter of fact he was sent to negotiate on the basis of Independence. No man has brought greater disasters to the interests of India than did Mr. Gandhi at the Round Table Conference. Less one speaks of him the better.

How far each of these interests feel satisfied with the Federal Scheme such as it is, it is not for me to say. The question one may however ask is, are these the only points of view that must be taken into consideration in deciding as to what we shall do with this Federation ? I protest that there are other points of view besides those mentioned above which must receive attention. There is the point of view of the Free man. There is also the point of view of the Poor man. What have they to say of Federation ? The Federation does not seem to take any account of them. Yet they are the people who are most deeply concerned. Can the free man hope that the Federal Constitution will not be a menace to his freedom ? Can the poor man feel that the constitution will enable him to have old values revalued, to have vested rights devested ? I have no doubt that this Federation if it comes into being will be a standing menace to the free man and an obstacle in the way of the poor man.

What freedom can there be when you are made subject to the autocracy of the Princes? What economic betterment can there be when you get Second Chambers with vested rights entrenched in full and when legislation affecting property is subject to sanction by the Government both before instroduction and after it has passed?

Conclusion.

I have perhaps detained you longer than I should have done. You will allow that it is not altogether my fault. The vastness of the subject is one reason for the length of this address.

I must, however, confess that there is also another reason which has persuaded me not to cut too short. We are standing today at the point of time where the old age ends and the new begins. The old age was the age of Ranade, Agarkar, Tilak, Gokhale, Wachha, Sir Pherozeshah Mehta, Surendranath Bannerjee. The new age is the age of Mr. Gandhi and this generation is said to be Gandhi generation. As one who knows something of the old age and also something of the new I see some very definite marks of difference between the two. The type of leadership has undergone a profound change. In the age of Ranade the leaders struggled to modernize India. In the age of Gandhi the leaders are making her a living specimen of antiquity. In the age of Ranade leaders depended upon experience as a corrective method of their thoughts and their deeds. The leaders of the present age depend upon their inner voice as their guide. Not only is there a difference in their mental make up there is a difference even in their view point regarding external appearance. The leaders of the old age took care to be well clad while the leaders of the present age take pride in being half clad. The leaders of the Gandhi age are of course aware of these differences. But far from blushing for their views and their appearance they claim that the India of Gandhi is superior to India of Ranade. They say that the age of Mr. Gandhi is an agitated and an expectant age, which the age of Mr. Ranade was not.

Those who have lived both in the age of Ranade and the age of Gandhi will admit that there is this difference between the two. At the same time they will be able to insist that if the India of Ranade was less agitated it was more honest and that if it was less expectant it was more enlightened. The age of Ranade was an age in which men and women did engage themselves seriously in studying and examining the facts of their life, and what is more important is that in the face of the opposition of the orthodox mass they tried to mould their lives and their character in accordance with the light they found as a result of their research. In the age of Ranade there was not the same divorce between a politician and a student which one sees in the Gandhi age. In the age of Ranade a politician, who was not a student, was treated as an intolerable nuisance, if not a danger. In the age of Mr. Gandhi learning, if it is not despised, is certainly not deemed to be a necessary qualification of a politician.

To my mind there is no doubt that this Gandhi age is the dark age of India. It is an age in which people instead of looking for their ideals in the future are returning to antiquity. It is an age in which people have ceased to think for themselves and as they have ceased to think they have ceased to read and examine the facts of their lives. The fate of an ignorant democracy which refuses to follow the way shown by learning and experience and chooses to grope in the dark paths of the mystics and the megalomaniacs is a sad thing to contemplate. Such an age I thought needed something more than a mere descriptive sketch of the Federal Scheme. It needed a treatment which was complete though not exhaustive and pointed without being dogmatic in order to make it alive to the dangers arising from the inauguration of the Federal Scheme. This is the task I had set before myself in preparing this address. Whether I have failed or suceeded, it is for you to say. If this address has length which is not compensated by depth, all I can say is that I have tried to do my duty according to my lights.

I am not opposed to a Federal Form of Government. I confess I have a partiality for a Unitary form of Government. I think India needs it. But I also realize that a Federal Form of Government is inevitable if there is to be Provincial Autonomy. But I am in dead horror the Federal Scheme contained in the Government of India Act. I think I have justified my antipathy by giving adequate reasons. I want all to examine them and come to their own conclusions. Let us however realize that the case of Provincial Autonomy is very different from that of the Federal Scheme. To those who think that the Federation should become acceptable if the Governor-General gave an assurance along the same lines as was supposed to be done by the Governors that he will not exercise his powers under his special responsibilities I want to say two things. First I am sure the Governor-General cannot give such an assurance because he is exercising these powers not merely in the interest of the Crown but also in the interest of the States. Secondly, even if he did, that cannot alter the nature of the Federal Scheme. To those who think that a change in the system of State representation from nomination to election will make the Federation less objectionable, I want to say that they are treating a matter of detail as though it was a matter of fundamental. Let us note what is fundamental and what is not. Let there be no mistake, let there be no fooling as to this. We have had enough of both. The real question is the extension and the growth of responsibility. Is that possible ? That is the crux. Let us also realize that there is no use hugging to Provincial Autonomy and leaving Responsibility in the Centre hanging in the air. I am convinced that without real responsibility at the Centre, Provincial Autonomy is an empty shell.

What we should do to force our point of view, this is no place to discuss. It is enough if I have succeeded in giving you an adequate idea of what are the dangers of this Federal Scheme.